*Of Mozart,*
*Parrots and*
*Cherry*
*Blossoms*
*in the Wind*

BRUCE ADOLPHE

# Of Mozart, Parrots and Cherry Blossoms in the Wind

A COMPOSER EXPLORES

MYSTERIES OF THE

MUSICAL MIND

LIMELIGHT EDITIONS • NEW YORK

First Limelight Edition, September 1999

Manufactured in the United States of America.


Library of Congress Cataloging-in-Publication Data

Adolphe, Bruce.
        Of Mozart, parrots, and cherry blossoms in the wind : a composer
    explores mysteries of the musical mind / Bruce Adolphe.
                    p.      cm.
        Includes index.
        ISBN 0-87910-286-1
        1. Music--Philosophy and aesthetics.  2. Music--Psychology.
    I. Title.
    ML3845.A36    1999
    781'.1--dc21                                    99-40618
                                                    CIP

*For Marija and Katja*

# ACKNOWLEDGEMENTS

GRATEFUL ACKNOWLEDGEMENTS AND THANKS TO Polly, Dan and Leo Weissman, and the Weissman Family Foundation for making this project possible; to Bantam Books, a division of Random House, Inc., for permission to quote from *True West* by Sam Shepard; to Jacqueline M. Taylor, Executive Director of the Chamber Music Society of Lincoln Center, for continually adding planks to my platform and pushing me closer to its edge where many of these essays were first heard as lectures; to David Shifrin, the Chamber Music Society's Artistic Director, who happily lets me try just about anything; to Mark Dichter, whom I cannot thank enough for his expert, ever-present camera, boundless energy and support; to Renée Tenenbaum for keeping our education department whirring without worrying; to David Finckel and Wu Han, who have graciously let me be part of their extraordinary projects; and to Mel Zerman, Mr. Limelight himself, for his trust, patience, encouragement and commitment.

# TABLE OF CONTENTS

# Table of Contents

*Of Mozart,*
*Parrots and*
*Cherry*
*Blossoms*
*in the Wind*

# Introduction

THE ESSAYS IN THIS BOOK are independent yet related, like piano etudes with a single opus number. Drawn primarily from my lectures at the Chamber Music Society of Lincoln Center, and also from talks I have given at music festivals and concert series around the country—including Summerfest La Jolla in California and Chamber Music Northwest in Oregon —the essays address the most provocative questions of audience members, as well as the typical concerns of professional musicians. Some of the themes that appear throughout the book are: Does music have meaning beyond sound? How does music communicate feelings and ideas? Does knowing *about* a piece affect the way we listen to it? How do composers get ideas? How does a composer think about musical form? How does memory feed the imagination? How can composing be taught? What does it mean when experts disagree? The most fundamental question of these essays is: How does a composer's life relate to his musical ideas?

Beyond addressing the questions and concerns of audiences and musicians, these essays reveal my own, personal and continually evolving ideas about the nature of creativity and the human need to discover meaning. I have increasingly become aware of and fascinated by the ways that my intense involvement with music has taught me about human nature and helped me to know my own mind. Like a novelist, whose real life and fictional creations are complexly intertwined, a composer both discovers and reinvents himself in his work.

Unlike the novelist, the composer does not deal with specific scenarios, but with metaphor and mystery. As a composer, I am interested in the relationship of my "real life" to my musical fictions. This book is an attempt to explore various mysteries of the musical mind: the partnership of memory and imagination; how technique embodies meaning; the counterpoint of intuition and intellect; and how we turn private life into public art. Along the way, we encounter not only the music of Mozart, Beethoven, Crumb and Takemitsu, but also the songs of parrots and whales, and the sound of cherry blossoms floating in the wind.

# Music's Deep Physics

"AT THE STILL POINT, THERE THE DANCE IS,"wrote T.S.Eliot, and he was right. The dance at the still point is not merely a poetic idea or a romantic notion. It is a fact of deep physics. The physicist Richard Feynman said, "What looks still to our crude eyes is a wild and dynamic dance." Feynman was referring to the bouncing about of atoms in a glass of water that has been covered and was sitting for days. Eliot was talking about the bouncing atoms at the center of our souls. They are the same atoms, of course, for there is only one kind in us, in water, in the rings of Saturn.

To write meaningful music, that is to say music that embodies a metaphor for experience, the composer must find that still point, and join the dance. This means leaving self-consciousness behind, forgetting to think *about* music but thinking *in* music. It means that we must vanish from the busy world, get small and rub up against some atoms. We must disappear into the universal mystery, where time does not tick but flows, where space is unbounded, where I can't tell *you* from *me*. We can describe this state of mind in prose, poetry, music and art forever and it can't be used up. The mountains may inspire infinite symphonies but none are the same, and the mountains don't care. The mystery is thoughtless, that is to say without thought. To discover its power, we must think so deeply that we lose our train of thought, we must derail it. Then we can find the quiet frenzy of pure intelligence. It's not knowing *about*, just knowing *that*. Children are good at this, especially when they play. This is not a place for politics or banking. It's the best place to make love, and music.

But it is not only the vanishing that matters. When we return to the common commotion, we have our work to do. Technique kicks in to record the trip, to notate that part of the dance we can remember, to capture a fragment of the universal hum. Technique is a net for catching idea fish. Technique gives us the tools for better listening and remembering, which leads to endless imagining. It's a circle.

We can practice listening, starting anywhere, with anything. Listen to a candle's flame flicker and the wax drop. Listen to the helpless pipes in the walls and the radiator's rude proclamations. I listen to my parrot rubbing his beak on his perch, always the same rhythm—and a good one. As any scientist knows, learning to observe closely is essential. It is all practice for getting down to musical atoms, where that still point is.

But observation is only the beginning. First we observe, then we imagine, and soon the mind wanders, and we let it go its own way. But we must follow it carefully, not interfering, like a detective following a suspect, careful not to be seen, watching but not predicting. If we simply follow, the suspect may indeed lead us across a dark street, down an alley, through a door, down some stairs to a still point, where some dancing is going on. It's a circle dance. It's quite a party, and some atoms are dancing to vibrating super strings. When I return home, I hope to make a full report.

# BODY LOOPS

Antonio damasio, neuroscientist and author of *Descartes'*
*Error,* coined the term "body loop" to mean the neural
path that emotions travel from "mind/brain to body and back
to mind/brain", as opposed to what he calls the "As if" loop,
triggered by a "bypass device", in which we "conjure up some
semblance of a feeling within the brain alone."

To a great extent, we recognize that emotions happen in
our bodies—not only in our minds—in our daily lives. The
triggers may appear anywhere. My father died when I was
eleven, and the things I associate with him can trigger my
body loop. The sight of an old *Rambler,* the car my father
drove, might bring tears to my eyes.

What role does the "body loop" play in the arts? In the
theater, actors train the "body loop" and practice tapping into
it. An actor who needs to portray emotions vividly and realistically must have those emotions available. But how to find
them? Among the many points of view on this, there are the
two interesting extremes. The argument might be phrased as
a question: *Which comes first, the feeling or the face?* Some
actors—I am thinking of Dustin Hoffman and Robert
DeNiro—work from emotional states. How the actor looks
to the audience is a result of that actor feeling the part. While
this may seem obvious, it is not the only way. Other actors—

here we may picture Lord Laurence Olivier—find the look first, expecting that the emotional life of the character will follow. Lord Olivier would put on the appropriate hat, look in the mirror and make the expression that seemed right, and the feelings that were suggested by the face in the mirror would soon arise. Often, both approaches come into play. The actor Karl Malden not only tried to imagine and feel the inner life of the true-life priest he portrayed in the film *On the Waterfront*, but he borrowed the real priest's hat and coat for the film, hoping for outside-in emotional magic. (It seems to have worked.) If a memory can loop through the body, why can't a body position stimulate the loop initially? Olivier would act in order to feel; DeNiro would feel in order to act.

Whether the feeling or the face comes first, the "body loop" clicks in, at least when the performers are at their best. Otherwise, "As if" acting will have to serve. For roles in opera or musical theater, the "As if" loop is usually employed rather than the more "real" "body loop" because of the necessity of precise musical timing and coordination with other singers and the orchestra, and because of dancing and a variety of extremely unrealistic activities that must take place during "acting." While an extremely talented and experienced actor in a drama may alter pacing, intonation and emphasis, an opera singer may not alter rhythm, pitch and prosody. But when a singer has performed a role often enough, it is possible that the portrayal will turn into total identification. The "As if" can stimulate the "body loop". When this happens, the performer will be exhausted at the end of the work. While this is an exhilarating experience for the performer (and probably for the audience), to perform in that "body" state night after night in a long run would be stressful, unhealthy and, for most performers, impossible.

What about emotional loops for instrumentalists and composers? Musicians in a string quartet, for example, do not deal with "portrayal" as do actors in a play. Their "script", the musical score, has no words (with some exceptions), and while it may be extremely emotional, the issues of motivation, action and situation are abstract, the meaning metaphorical.

But musicians know that while the recognizable real-life situations in a movie or play are more specific, they are not necessarily more precise than music. We tend to link words to the idea of understanding. But the idea that if you cannot *name* something, you do not *know* it, is false. The act of articulation, of naming and describing, often sets up artificial parameters and draws borders around *knowing* that devalue what cannot be verbally defined. The accurate articulation of any phenomenon gives a sensation of joy that can be called understanding, but we must be mindful of the profoundly inexpressible remainder.

String quartet players, as in any chamber ensemble, must negotiate and coordinate a complex network of technical tasks in the service of a musical concept. The concept undoubtedly involves emotions that run deep, triggered by the music. But unlike an actress portraying a mother in grief over her son's murder, a violinist playing an emotionally charged melody in a late quartet of Beethoven has no single scenario to enact. Yet, the violinist can identify with the music, become it, and tap into a nonverbal ocean of experience and emotion.

Eugene Drucker, violinist with the Emerson String Quartet, told me that he has experienced real "body loop" emotions during performances, causing physical reactions. During one performance of the slow movement of Beethoven's string quartet Opus 59, No. 1, Drucker found himself thinking of his mother, who died when he was twelve. His sadness became so strong that he began to cry quietly while playing. He didn't want the introspection and tragic atmosphere of the slow movement to give way, as it must, to the high spirits and manic energy of the Finale. Drucker has also been nearly overwhelmed while performing the *Cavatina* from Beethoven's Opus 130 as well as the slow movement of Debussy's String Quartet. He states, however, that he did not lose awareness of the music, or of playing it during these episodes. The physically and intellectually complex tasks involved in playing this music on the violin, and performing with his colleagues in the Emerson Quartet, continued while his memories, triggered emotionally, wandered. But were they wandering away from or *into* the music?

When Marcel Proust's housekeeper, Celeste, said that she read literature because novels "take me out of myself", Proust replied, "But novels should take you into yourself."

Can the audience tell whether a musician has entered the "body loop" or not? While some members of the audience professed to being profoundly moved during the episodes Eugene Drucker described, they have also been equally moved when the performers felt no particular connections to extramusical events. It is far more typical for musicians to be emotionally engaged with only the music itself, without associations to specific life experiences. This is the most common state for performers. In fact, it is the ability and tendency to connect to music purely and profoundly, without conscious extramusical associations, that leads to a lifetime of involvement with the art. But those associations are, nonetheless, present, as any performer (or listener) who has suddenly and unexpectedly entered the "body loop" knows.

For a composer, the question of inspiration can pose similar issues. Does one have a feeling that is then transformed into notes and rhythm, or does one improvise music which gives rise to feelings? Both can happen. The same loop of memory and metaphor may be approached from either direction, as with actors.

The memory of an emotional event can spark, in the mind of a composer, a musical idea. Thinking about the feeling of restlessness I have had at night, remembering the inability to sleep, the tossing and turning, gave me a very physical sensation which, in turn, suggested a rhythmic idea, a tempo and even a pattern of notes swirling in a kind of elliptical design. This restless music became the opening of my second string quartet. Once I began to compose the quartet, all thoughts about sleeplessness disappeared. In fact, all verbal thoughts, what could be thought of as *programmatic* ideas, vanished, as they must, in order to compose. For me, even when music is inspired or triggered by extramusical events, the process of composing is always absolute and pure. A composer thinks *in* sound, not *about* it. This thinking in sound is informed by ideas of musical order and syntax gained through listening, writing, study and experience. After ideas are formed clearly, *then* it is a good idea to "step back" from the music, to think *about* it. This allows one to edit and make choices that elevate the music beyond a kind of improvisation, to bring it to the higher ground of composition. While composing the quartet, I had forgotten about the sleeplessness and the initial impulse for the opening of the work. It was only after completing the final draft, when I thought the piece might benefit from a suggestive title, that I remembered, and decided to call it *Turning, Returning.* The title refers not only to my turning my body over in bed, but to turning an idea around in my mind, re-turning it, and returning *to* it.

Frequently, however, I must compose on a schedule in order to meet a deadline, a fact of professional life. Composing on a schedule often requires a different approach to the loop.

Instead of allowing events, emotions or memories to suggest musical ideas, I might jump-start the process by improvising music, allowing the music to trigger emotions. In such cases, I will eventually stumble upon a musical pattern that jolts my memory, provoking the loop. Soon I will find myself trying to capture a strong emotion conjured up by those improvised notes. Once captured, that group of notes becomes a purely musical entity, and the composing can proceed as before. Another way I enter the loop is by picking up a recently finished work of mine, and treating it as though it were not finished. It is like stepping into a play and changing some essential lines or action. This allows the finished piece to function like an event from life, just as though the piece were a memory that sparks new ideas. The process of composing is always, for me, a balance of two states of mind/body: emotional, fevered, inspired; thoughtful, detached, analytical. Either may come first, and often they exist simultaneously, in a counterpoint of mind.

The initial inspiration for a work may occur while daydreaming about music or, quite unexpectedly, while in the midst of some unrelated activity. The thoughtful, analytical part of composing is always done purposely, sitting at a piano or desk. This process might be described as the attempt to physically capture inspired ideas—it feels like remembering a dream—and the subsequent attempt to understand and realize the implications of those ideas. As with a dream, trying to remember often generates new ideas. They are welcome, since it is all part of the same adventure.

In the midst of an analysis of a passage of music (Is it clear? Does it flow from the previous phrase? Does it sit well on the instrument? How should I divide a chord among the instruments? Is the phrase long enough or short enough to be convincing?), an idea, which has the feeling of a *solution*, will occur. Finding a solution to a problem is emotionally uplifting, and it may give rise to memories and feelings that in turn lead to another technical problem. Loops.

In my composition *Body Loops*, for piano and orchestra, I clearly began composing in the "As if" loop, thinking of how the feeling of emotions might be portrayed in rhythms, harmonies and timbres. After I jotted down musical phrases,

I began to improvise with them, and the act of physical performance stirred stronger emotions. These emotions then fed my improvisation, which led to revising the initial musical phrases. I decided to keep various versions or "states" of the music in the piece, to make the conflicting versions the point of the work. The result is a structural loop uniting varied levels of emotional intensity in the presentation of a single idea. It is not a theme with variations, but rather a series of *versions* of an idea, none of which has dominance. There can be no authentic version. To me this is a kind of musical realism: *Memory* itself is the theme.

Antonio Damasio points out that an emotion in the "body loop" is "constructed anew, moment by moment, and is not an exact replica of anything that happened before." Memories, too, he explains, are "attempts at replication". When we remember, we construct, patterns converge, hopefully resembling the "original" as we perceived it, however inaccurate *that* may have been.

In a sense, memory always involves an element of fiction. We are all writers of our own stories, which are in a constant state of revision. The composer Maurice Ravel's thoughts about inspiration and originality are particularly interesting in this context. Ravel commented that if a composer has nothing to say, he would "do well to repeat what has been well said." He added that if a composer does have something to say, it will emerge from his "unwitting infidelity to the model." In other words, "originality" in music (or any art) is like the fiction of memory that results when we attempt to reconstruct an exact replica. We can't help being creative: that is how our minds work. The challenge is to recognize our particular fictions, to capture them as best we can and to present them clearly, like dreams told well. How can we tell which fictions are worth telling? Listen to the "body loop".

# Everything Matters:

## THE REAL LIFE OF HARMONY, MELODY, AND COUNTERPOINT

MUSICIANS IN REHEARSAL WILL DISCUSS what "to bring out", which line is most important and how to balance the dynamics of an ensemble. Listeners tend to focus on the foreground, which usually means melody. This is all quite natural. But the best musicians and listeners understand that in music, as in life, *everything* matters.

The tunes and themes that demand so much attention are most often derived from the harmony, from what is commonly thought to be the *background*, and are pulled like single threads from whole cloth. Melodies, in most music since the late Renaissance, arise from harmony, and seek *new* harmonies like children leaving home to discover the world. The idea that harmony is merely a background to melody makes me think of children who, quite naturally, view all grownups as part of a vague backdrop to their own center-stage performances.

A good cook will also understand that *everything*—all the elements and ingredients—is essential. It's so often the sauce, more than the meat or fish, that determines the success of a dish. How often do we decide what to order in a restaurant based on what "comes with" the main course? When we think of the elements of music in terms of "real life", we begin to appreciate how much *everything* matters.

Movie directors certainly understand this, both visually and in terms of sound. A director has to decide how important background noises are to create a certain ambiance. Imagine two hikers talking casually about bears as they make their way up a grassy mountainside. What do you hear? In the foreground: the conversation. But what other sounds are there? The hikers' footsteps crunch grass, crack twigs, pat the soft patches of earth; what about the cries of finches, starlings, crows, or the flapping wings of a hawk overhead? Water in a stream near the path rushes by, a squirrel or chipmunk, or maybe a snake, causes a whoosh in the bush; the wind through the trees, the sudden mosquito at your ear. How much should the director capture with his microphone; how much to keep or discard; how loud should this atmosphere be? While sitting in the dark theater, do we pay attention to the film's background sounds? What effect does it have? The background sounds can produce an ironic counterpoint to the foreground dialogue, creating an eerie, threatening atmosphere around the innocent conversation.

Living in the city, we unconsciously learn to block out background. Too-sensitive car alarms, drive-by radios, Doppler-ing sirens, fragments of quarrels, and the squeals of garbage truck brakes, sounding like the last gasps of wounded animals, combine nightly in a terrible polyphony, causing sleeplessness and tension headaches — or causing dreams to take bizarre turns that baffle therapists the following morning.

We may gain an ability to concentrate amid noisy distractions, but we lose a great deal when we tune out the world. An egotistical soloist, who ignores the orchestra, may play his part brilliantly, but he will ruin the concerto. When we turn up the volume of our own channel and lower the reception of the world around us, we train ourselves to ignore, to undermine, to underestimate, and not to care.

One composer who heard the world's chatter and noise as if it were music, is Leoš Janáček. To Janáček, a musical accompaniment was no mere strumming, no Alberti bass, no oom-pah-pah. There were no second-class musical citizens in his domain. A subsidiary musical figure was no more to be understood as mere background than the wind's whisper or hawk's beating wings are accompaniments to human activity. Janáček loved nature and animals. He studied all the sounds that he heard as music, including human speech. The composer took dictation on the street: Overheard reproaches, greetings, laments and laughter were fixed in distinct rhythms, exact pitches and marked forte or piano in his musical diaries. Janáček recorded a conversation with Smetana's daughter on paper as operatic recitative.

He understood the polyphonic nature of the world, that there is melody, harmony and counterpoint everywhere. Janáček captured the music of a bursting water pipe. He committed to his musical notebook the complaints of crows, the arguments of finches and the warnings and premonitions of his three pet hens, whom he called Mrs. Bila, Mrs. Kovalska and Mrs. Slavkovska. He notated as music the seething waves and the collision of clouds. In his notebooks, he captured the "bloodthirsty nocturne" of a mosquito.

And conversely, for Janáček, every note, every chord had life, purpose, a mission. Janáček wrote, "For me, a chord is being come alive: a bloodstained flower of the musical art. I know when I write it that pain grips my heart; that the heart moans, wails, falls hard on the ground, crushes, is fragmented by the mist, hardens into granite."

This kind of musical realism can affect the way one listens to the music of "real life". And this, in turn, can deepen one's ability to comprehend layers of activity in music. Imagine that you are listening to your friend on the phone as she invites you to dinner, but, suddenly, you hear a man yelling in the next-door apartment and the sounds of a television drama coming from above. Or perhaps you are thinking of what you'll have for dinner as you walk down the street past a homeless woman who is digging through the trash for hers. Is she the background to your walk? Can you see yourself, for a moment, as the background in her drama? Later on, at the restaurant, you are telling a story, but you hear someone at another table whispering about someone you know, and suddenly you find yourself listening to him instead of yourself.

The counterpoint of real life has affected the music of many composers. In a single meeting with Freud in 1910, Gustav Mahler discovered why, in so much of his music, he had a tendency to interrupt the most profound, noble music with trivial tunes — an aspect of his work considered moving and *realistic* by many music lovers, but which Mahler himself considered a weakness. Mahler's father mistreated his mother regularly. During a particularly brutal argument between his parents when he was a little boy, Mahler ran from the house into the street. There, the atmosphere was suddenly commonplace, as a hurdy-gurdy played the popular tune "Ach, du lieber Augustin".

Mahler felt that the simple, popular melody and the anguish in his heart were forever linked in his mind. Tragedy and triviality, a juxtaposition common in real life, became a uniquely realistic aspect of Mahler's musical grammar.

Mahler's music is itself a catalyst for Luciano Berio's extraordinary *Sinfonia* of 1969, for large orchestra and eight amplified voices. The Italian composer created a web of music and words which negates the concepts of foreground, middleground and background, creating instead a shockingly recognizable tangle of ideas, suggesting the way thoughts and images flow through the mind when we try to remember the distant past. Berio chose to use the entire *Scherzo* from Mahler's Second Symphony within his own symphony. Berio explained that in the third movement of *Sinfonia*, Mahler's music flows "through a constantly changing landscape, sometimes going underground and emerging in another, altogether different place, sometimes disappearing completely, present either as a fully recognizable form or as small details lost in the surrounding host of musical presences." In addition to musical quotes, Berio sets texts as diverse as a meditation on Martin Luther King, Brazilian myths about the origin of water as analyzed by Claude Levi-Strauss and Samuel Beckett's *The Unnameable*. Often compared to Joyce's *Finnegans Wake*, *Sinfonia* sounds as if we were somehow listening to someone's mind, as ideas and memories of music and texts rush forward and recede, now vivid, now elusive, converging now and then in meaningful association. It is extremely realistic music in its embodiment of mental processes.

There is a particular kind of real-life music that occurs when two people are trying to tell a story at once. At dinner tables and parties around the world, this is an all-too-familiar experience. You hear what *could* be a linear narrative in a jumble of highlights and fragments, peppered with contradictions. "Are you going to let me tell this or not?" is a common cry. Or perhaps the listener says, "One at a time! I can't follow this!" But to a composer, it is all music — a story told in conversational counterpoint, richly textured, provocative and active. It is, musically speaking, a kind of heterophony — the splitting of a single line into versions of itself, like an image in a broken mirror. There is no background, no foreground.

The meaning of music begins with the daily hums and clicks around us. A friend tells you about her day while accompanying herself with a virtuosic display of garlic chopping, the knife moving like a violinist's bow in rapid spicatto movements. Rossini, a composer with an ear for the comedy of chatter, would have appreciated the counterpoint of our urban coffee bars — people simultaneously calling out "one decaf tall cappuccino to go", "grande latte with 2 per-cent milk for here" or "a grande Americano iced".

More and more, I find myself imagining the music of real life: the melodic curve of a suggestive smile; the stinging dissonance of an angry glance; the startling music of a huge yellow moon caught between skyscrapers. What is important? All of it.

# AND ALL IS ALWAYS NOW:

## SOME THOUGHTS ON STRUCTURE AND COUNTERPOINT

W E LIVE IN CONSTANT COUNTERPOINT. As millions of people drive home from work, they listen to the radio and simultaneously think about the day's events, plan dinner, ponder a range of personal matters, perhaps talk on the car phone, and somehow manage not to drive off the road or get into an accident. Counterpoint is the natural condition of the human mind. Our memories, dreams, plans, obsessions, hopes, present thoughts, new ideas and imaginings all exist now in the mind. It is that *now* that T.S. Eliot refers to in the phrase, "And all is always now..."

That is a modern idea of counterpoint, which has had many meanings throughout the history of music. The ancient *ricercare* was, as the name suggests, a form of musical "research" in which the composer sought to discover everything knowable about a given "subject" or musical idea. The *ricercare* was a single-minded, uncompromising process: a rigorous exploration of a single motif—more like a pinecone than a graduate student. The art of fugue, as practiced by Johann Sebastian Bach, was a spiritual endeavor. The subject can be heard as a kind of protagonist, while the fugal design gives a sense that the protagonist is a pawn in Destiny's great plan. The chorale prelude gives us a counterpoint of angels and mortals: the slow, ethereal soprano statements of the chorale, hovering high above the hustle-bustle tempo of the work-a-day choir. In opera, counterpoint has been realistically employed to give conflicting points of view from the stage or to portray the natural counterpoint of real-life scenes, such as crowds, parties, meals, and so on. Rossini apparently liked to compose amidst lots of babble, and he would invite people over to his rooms for that purpose.

As natural as it is, counterpoint has not always been well thought of. Rousseau articulated the general feeling of his time when he wrote in his *Lettre sur la musique française* (1753):

"With regard to counterfugues, double fugues, inverted fugues, ground basses, and other difficult sillinesses that the ear cannot abide and which reason cannot justify, these are obviously remnants of barbarism and bad taste that only persist, like the portals of our Gothic cathedrals to the shame of those who had the endurance to build them."

The new Classical style had rejected counterpoint, along with complexities of harmony and melody, in favor of a simpler, narrative approach to musical form. A movement in a Baroque piece would typically explore one emotion or *affectation*, giving the sense of an inward emotional spiral rather than a linear journey of action. By contrast, the many masterpieces created by Haydn, Mozart, early Beethoven and others in the Classical style are generally structured as musical scenarios, where themes are like characters, keys are locations and modulations are dramatic changes of scene. It is, of course, possible to hear such works as *internal* dramas rather than as scenarios of external action, but their essential nature is still narrative and linear.

To me, the procedures of sonata form strongly resemble a courtroom trial. The opening themes (especially if the work is in a minor key) may be heard as arguments of the prosecution and defense; the development tends to sound like arguments, objections, cross-examinations, and, frequently, the presentation of new evidence; the recapitulation is the summing up and final statements; the coda is the announcement of the verdict and sentencing. As in real life, this outline is very compelling, and it is a powerful way to get to the heart (or truth) of an infinity of human dramas.

In the late works of Beethoven, the classical linear (courtroom) drama concept begins to give way to a more varied and flexible approach to compositional forms. (Perhaps he had seen enough of the courtroom during battles over the custody of his nephew!) It appears as though Beethoven had lost interest in the constraints of the courtroom dialectic and, instead, wanted a new kind of emotional immediacy. He was a musical vigilante, impatient with the conventional forces of law and order. Beethoven, in what now some ironically might call a post-modernist frame of mind, restored some of the Baroque concepts and procedures to the art. He integrated, for example, fugue, dance forms and recitative with variations and sonata. In his Opus 132 string quartet, Beethoven returns to the long forgotten texture of the chorale prelude, transforming the spiritual (almost theological) texture into a profoundly personal message.

Much has been written about Beethoven's return to counterpoint, but what concerns me more here is a counterpoint of a different nature: Beethoven discovered the counterpoint of conflicting states of mind. This is the counterpoint implied by T.S. Eliot's phrase *And all is always now*. There exists (particularly in the first movements of Op.109, 130 and 132) a music of interruption, of splintered attention. In a manner that conjures up the psychotherapist's technique of free association, it is music of contrasts, confusion and connections. One way to hear this music is as an exposition of the creative process itself, as if Beethoven were allowing the listener to hear how his mind works. This is a believable explanation of the first movement of the string quartet Opus 130. Heard this way, the exposition of this movement — to use conventional sonata terminology—is a search for musical ideas. We are permitted to listen as Beethoven attempts to focus on the most worthy of a multitude of musical thoughts that appear in his mind without conscious effort. The development, then, is the conscious integration of these ideas into a clear structure. The recapitulation is an unraveling of the development, to remind us of how the trick was done. (The irony is, of course, that it took a lot of work for Beethoven to give the *impression*, in the exposition, of free association and of a mind at play.)

Before these conceptual and structural innovations, sonata was primarily a linear form. Beethoven uncovered a process of emotional spirals and loops, a music of split consciousness, multi-layered and immediate. It is not a counterpoint of simultaneous melodic lines, but of conflicting psychological states. This "realistic" portrayal of the contrapuntal action of the human mind is the main element that makes the late works of Beethoven seem modern, even today. This has inevitably led to a freedom from received forms, giving us the personal musical visions of generations of composers.

Thinking and learning about the contrapuntal nature of the mind inspires in me a particular kind of musical thinking, especially in my darker pieces. It has occurred to me that my personality is contrapuntal. Quick to joke and pun (too quick, sometimes), I often think simultaneously of quite serious things. In my piece *And All Is Always Now* for violin and piano, I have tried to capture the "split-screen" of emotions we all experience. The music has several layers that do not appear in simultaneous counterpoint, but rather suddenly emerge to dominate, much as I experience in daily life. The work was recently performed in Portland, Oregon, at the Chamber Music Northwest festival. The festival's executive director sat at my left in the audience. After the performance, she turned to me and asked, "Where does the violence come from in that piece? You're such a funny, easy-going guy!" I answered without hesitation. I told her about the accident to my right wrist in 1974, when I was nineteen. A shattered piece of glass cut through my ulnar nerve, all the tendons in four fingers and the main artery. I almost died. I also told her about three people I knew who had been murdered: a next-door neighbor in a big apartment building in New York, and two violinists—one by her husband near Marlboro and the other backstage at the Metropolitan Opera. Both violinists were thrown to their deaths—I had terrifying dreams of falling for months afterward. Hours after the concert, I continued to think about the violence in the music. I thought about my parents, both of whom died when I was young—my father when I was eleven, and my mother when I was nineteen. But when I thought about my life at the time when *And All Is Always Now* was composed, I realized that it was shortly after a bitter divorce. My wife was a dancer who had been having an affair with a dancer in her company (which toured a great deal) during the entire year that we had been married. Before I found this out, her lover thought nothing of borrowing money from me, eating dinner with us and asking my advice about his problems. When it all blew up, I had violent dreams, not only at night, but it affected my daydreams as well. I would be riding on a train, and a dream of horrible, fierce revenge would appear in my mind, full of detail, including the ensuing courtroom trial.

Images of gruesome violence would suddenly appear in my mind at any time, no matter what I was doing. Perhaps Adorno had something when he wrote, "Every work of art is an un-committed crime."

In thinking about where the violence came from in *And All Is Always Now*, I realized that, six years after composing the piece, I had forgotten the immediate cause. In listening to the piece in concert, I was concerned only with the music, not at all with its relationship to real events in my life. Certainly, the audience does not need to know anything about my life to relate to the work's structure of lyricism and violence. It is probably better that they not know the story behind the music, because ignorance of the real-life drama allows them to feel and think about the music in terms of their own experiences rather than mine. Music is not meant to be an illustration of events, and there is the danger that a score could be heard as movie music without the movie.

With some of my music, however, I have tried the other approach. My piano concerto, *After the End*, was composed just after that particular crisis in my life, and the title refers directly to the end of that relationship and the beginning of a new one. I provided program notes for the audience that revealed the whole story with some detail. The press in Jacksonville, Florida, where the work was premiered, went to town with this information. They promoted the work as a big soap-opera scenario turned into a piano concerto by a wild composer during fits of desperation. In spite of this tasteless build-up, the audience was seriously moved, and many people told me that knowing the true story helped them to enter the world of the music and to follow its form. The seven-movement structure of this work is quite complex, with many changes of tempo and subtle variations of ideas. Perhaps the audience would have been confused by the work had they not had a real-life drama on which to fix their attention. One man grabbed my arm during intermission and said, "You could have been writing about me. It sounded like my life."

Musical structures are the shapes of our memories. Speculating on the real-life genesis of a musical form may be intriguing, but it is in the nature of music itself that we can never be sure if we are correct. Even composers cannot be certain. The musical work takes on its own truth, a metaphorical truth that is larger than any incident that may have inspired its creation. I did not need to uncover the specific incident that brought violence into counterpoint with lyricism to write the work, nor is it necessary to appreciate it. One often writes music without any idea of how it relates to daily events. A composer's life and music co-exist in a mysterious counterpoint.

In Arthur Miller's play *Death of a Salesman*, time and memory flow in a contrapuntal design that perfectly captures the complexity of the concept "and all is always now." The play takes place in the transitionless world of dream-time, as Willy Loman's memories appear and transform the action on the stage. The location of the drama is the protagonist's mind. Miller himself explained that he was inspired to write in this manner, partly, by his uncle, Manny Newman. Miller described his uncle as "living in two places at the same time." He said that his uncle had no boundaries between his memory and his present experience. Miller put it perfectly: "It's all now. And to me that was wonderful."

For me now, musical structures are linked to ideas of awareness and attention. The unexpected musical cues that suddenly trigger an emotional change or a new tempo seem very potent and real-to-life. My musical structures (when not dealing with a narrative piece) are formed from the feeling of memories, from the effort to recall something clearly, from frustrating emotional loops and thrilling shudders of recognition—from the counterpoint of memory and imagination. Musical structures reflect the understanding that all passion, pain, joy, obsessions, desires, fears, plans, dreams and hopes —even those we cannot remember—are always now in the mind.

# How Music Means

THE MEANING OF MUSIC has long been a difficult subject, for musicians especially. Musicians often say that music means nothing outside of itself, that music simply is. Many excellent composers have insisted that their works mean nothing beyond the notes, but this only confirms that they are better off writing the notes themselves than about notes. The stance that music means nothing but itself is an avoidance of the very idea of meaning by those who are worried that music will in some way be debased or devalued by an attempt to *translate* it into another language or medium. Certainly, music cannot be translated, but that is not the purpose of the search for meaning. Some musicians, who refuse to admit that music means anything, confuse the idea of representationalism with meaning.

To say that Debussy's *La Mer* (*The Sea*) is about the sea, or that it sounds like the sea, is not to say that it means the sea. A typical argument against meaning: if you change the name of the title from *The Sea* to, say, *Unrequited Love* (or many other possible titles), it would suit the music just as well and therefore the music is not really about the sea and therefore the music can mean anything and therefore it means nothing. What this argument conveniently ignores is that suit the music (not necessarily equally well), there are also many titles that would obviously be *inappropriate*. In order that a new programmatic title fit the music by Debussy, it must suggest certain qualities that are embodied by that music. It would be ludicrous to call the work *Sunset* or *Sunday in the Park*. The title *Unrequited Love* could work for the piece because, like the sea, it suggests qualities of restlessness, uncertainty, turmoil, even helplessness. Debussy's *La Mer* may, indeed, be about the sea on one level, but its meaning is deeper—it is metaphorical.

If a piece of music is performed, and no one gets its meaning, does it have any? Is Bach's *Art of the Fugue* meaningless if no one is left alive who "understands" it? Is it not possible that the piece embodies ideas of order, proportion, balance, wholeness and beauty that can be discovered by serious listening, just as anthropologists and linguists can discover the meaning of ancient symbols from a lost culture? Cannot those ideas of order, proportion, balance, wholeness and beauty then stimulate thought about universal questions, such as humanity's place in nature, in the universe? Those fugues, by the ways a subject is rigorously explored, suggest that there is something larger than the self (subject), and the sense of a "destiny that shapes our ends" is integral to Bach's contrapuntally conceived theology. At what point is this *meaning*?

Bach's *Art of the Fugue* embodies a worldview through its relatedness of details to the whole, its deep organizational principles, including its unity of horizontal (melodic) and vertical (harmonic) movement, its rhythmic elegance and its particular balance of dissonance and consonance. Debussy's *La Mer* captures the energy of the sea which, in turn, is *itself* understood as a metaphor for our own restless loneliness, a thrilling vastness and nameless uncertainty.

A famous composer, whose works I admire, said to me that he believed that music means nothing outside of itself. I then told him about my fourth string quartet, *Whispers of Mortality.* This work was composed as a reaction to the news that a good friend had developed a serious form of cancer. I explained that the quartet's five movements explored aspects of my friend's personality, as well as issues arising from his illness. The first movement, I told him, was built on music of shock and denial, with the first violin playing music of rage, while the other three instruments continued as if nothing had happened. In the second movement, I developed a melodic structure that I hoped would suggest a desire to go backward in time, prior to the disease. The music unfolded in a series of short phrases. With each new phrase, I added music *at the beginning* rather than at the end, which is normally done. This, I hoped, would *feel* like going backward, a common wish in the face of distress. I continued to describe the work as moving from shock and denial to struggling and, eventually, acceptance. In each movement, I searched for musical procedures that would suggest the emotional outline of the real-life drama. The famous composer said that I could just as well say that the piece is about a field of gazelles who were suddenly put upon by a hunter. An audience, he explained, would hear the music as a story of animals in distress, if I told them that *that* was what the music was about. Of course, they would believe me, but it would not be true. But, more importantly, his story of gazelles being hunted has the same emotional energy and shape as the true story of my friend's cancer. A discussion of particular scenarios points up music's universal nature, its ability to connect with profound experiences through the embodiment of emotional resonance.

The formation and recognition of meaning is the most significant activity of the human mind—it is the linking up of our neural networks, the confirmation of intuition, the completion of a circuit, energy spreading throughout the brain. Meaning is the cross-referencing of the various symbols —music, words, images—causing the mind to light up with recognition. Meaning is bridge-building, connecting memories and symbols through metaphor. The metaphors excited by artistic triggers are deep-grooved; they are the very networks formed during early learning.

Works of art, including music, have meaning if those works embody the *qualities of those deep metaphors*. Meaning in music is not a matter of assigning a scenario to a composition, but of recognizing, even if wordlessly, that a single piece of music may suggest an infinity of scenarios that are, in turn, specific versions of a metaphor. Music is not a particular action from daily life, but the resonance of action. Music is not a description of a memory, but rather the shape of memory. It may be that music mirrors the actions of the brain as it creates memory. Music, I suspect, is an expression of the way the brain becomes mind.

# THE GENETIC AND ENVIRONMENTAL
# ASPECTS OF MUSICAL COMPOSTION

UNTIL THE MODERN ERA of fluid and flexible compositional techniques, composers wrote music in closed systems (tonality, for example) in which all artistic decisions
were to some extent determined by the nature of the system.
If we think of tonality (being "in a key", such as C Major) as
the musical equivalent to DNA, then it follows that the musical work may be thought of as a particular living organism—
a human being, for example. Just as DNA contains all the
genetic information, the limitations and the potentialities, of
a human being, conceived by two parent human beings, a system such as tonality defines the possibilities of a musical piece
conceived (in tonality) by its composer. Just as genetic engineering makes it possible to change the nature of an organism, in simple ways and in ways we can only imagine at this
time, composers since the late nineteenth century have engi-
neered permutations, mutations, corruptions, deviations and
modifications of the once all-defining tonal system.

Any musical system of composition—including modes
from anywhere in the world—can be viewed as a kind of
DNA for unborn musical compositions. A work composed in
a Japanese mode cannot give us a Mozartian melody any
more than Mozart could conceive a Japanese, Indian or

within a system is  like genetics: even with all of Mozart's desire, imagination and willpower, he and his wife Constanza could not possibly make an Asian baby.

The tonal system developed in Western music, in use in various manifestations for over 400 years, is one of the world's most highly developed artistic modes of thought. Its deep patterning and infinite permutations (still within the system), comprise supple and complex methods of harmonic, contra-puntal, melodic and formal expression. Just as the history of genetics is not only one of science but also of social science, since the habits and patterns of human procreation alter the nature of the gene pool, the development of music requires the study of both compositional systems and individual com-posers.

My baby daughter's body—from her respiratory and cir-culatory systems, her neural network and vital organs to her skin and hair color—was determined by a particular set of genes from my wife and me, and from all our ancestors. How we raise her, and how her experiences with other humans affect her, will determine her personality only in part, for the genetic code gives us a particular human being right from the start.  Even more to the point, she cannot grow up to be a horsie or duckie, no matter how much she may want to, nor can Zen meditation, Bhuddist instruction, vegetarian diets or yoga alter the Jewish genetic code, with its particular risks and benefits, that she will pass on to her children.  So, too, every aspect of a work of Mozart, for example, can be accounted for by the tonal system itself as well as the genius of the compos-er. Mozart could conceive of brilliant modulations, delightful melodies, comic turns of phrase, tragic harmonies and elaborate contrapuntal tapestries; but the tonal system that allowed for all of this could not produce the dizzy Sephardic melody that I danced to with my parents when I was a child.

The tonal system of *diatonic* (notes of the key and its scale) and *chromatic* (notes foreign to the key, or "colorations" of it) tones is remarkably like the systems of living organisms. If we imagine that the diatonic condition is the human being at birth, we may imagine that the chromatic tones are the viruses, bacteria and other foreign entities that may invade the body.

Just as viral and bacterial invasion is inevitable and a normal part of being alive, so, too, chromatic intrusion into the diatonic body is the normal state of the life of a musical composition. We might even think of sneezes, coughs, burps and the rest of the all-too-common interruptions of our daily existence as the basic non-harmonic tones of life, the simple dissonances such as appoggiaturas and suspensions that we accept without raising an eyebrow or even so much as a *Gesundheit*. But when the little chromatic notes become more frequent, when flats begin to appear everywhere in C Major, like constant sneezes or chronic coughing, we can expect to be completely taken over by E-flat Major or C Minor, like a cold or flu that makes us keenly aware of how we take our health (C Major) for granted. This altered state is only temporary, and we can expect to be ourselves, in C Major that is, pretty soon, or at least by the end of the piece, even if we don't see a doctor. This is not saying that a change of key represents a disease in a piece of music, but, rather, that the music is not in the normal condition (tonic or "home" key), and that the new key is, structurally speaking, a dissonance that requires resolution, according to the system.

If we depart momentarily from the biological metaphor, we can demonstrate the tonal system's completeness with a similar metaphor: that of place. If a key is a country, then we may call the chromatic notes foreigners. These foreigners may wander through the key as passing tones, or they may be diplomats from near or distant keys. As diplomats, the chromatic tones may give the feeling of another key, in just a phrase, without the music actually having to change keys. But there may also be chromatic spies—double agents who exist in two keys at once. Just when you thought that you were visiting a friendly F-natural, you discover that he is an E-sharp, and you are whisked away to B Minor against your will. You will, of course, be rescued in the recapitulation, and the story will end in the home key.

With Wagner, Schumann, Chopin and the other revolutionaries of Romanticism, music became more chromatic, which is to say that diatonicism became unstable. Biologically, we might say that the gene pool was changing due to the chromatic promiscuity of these oh-so-romantic composers. To combine the biological metaphor with that of place, we could say that people traveled more, lived in different countries, brought back different foods and clothes, and even married foreigners. This led to a pervasive chromatic diversity, creating a population (i.e. the music) of increasingly mixed background.

With Debussy, Scriabin, Rimsky-Korsakov and other

visionary composers, we saw a period of further experimentation parallel to genetic engineering. Alternative modes were mixed in musical test tubes, symmetrical intervallic patterns were tested as replacements for the deeply ingrained circle of fifths, for years assumed to be necessary to the creation of musical organisms. Then Arnold Schoenberg forced the issue with a totally chromatic strand of DNA. This chromatic DNA determined all aspects of the organism, and blocked patterns derived from the old tonal DNA. His system was completely methodical and closed. Many composers became disciples while even more opposed it, declaring this form of genetic engineering to be dangerous and unnatural. Schoenberg pointed out, like any scientist, that if he had not discovered this system, some one else would have.

Since that time, the development of music, like science, has proceeded with unprecedented rapidity. Techniques of grafting, collage, transplantation and cloning have altered the musical landscape. With technology added to the phenomenon of genetically altered music, the future is a blank screen, indeed. Composers today can create musical creatures that Mozart could not even have imagined, the musical gene pool having been so profoundly altered since that time.

What will the future bring? The only sensible prediction is that no matter what technique or system may evolve or appear, music will continue to embody metaphors for human experience. The more *things* change, the more things change. But we remain the same.

# WHAT DID MOZART KNOW?

PERHAPS THE MOST FREQUENTLY ASKED QUESTION in the many music classes I have taught is: "Did Mozart (or Stravinsky, or any composer under discussion) know that he was doing that?" The "that" refers to a particularly subtle or richly complex aspect of the musical design, something extraordinary, inspiring and beautiful that I had just described. Another way to phrase the question is: "Was Mozart *thinking* about the technical aspects of the music, or writing down what he *heard* in his imagination?"

What causes this question to be asked so often? It usually arises when I point out to a class, for example, that in a piece by Mozart, we find a melodic fragment from the opening that is "hidden" later on in the work. The fragment is then slowed down, and chords are generated above each note of the tune, transforming it into a harmonic accompaniment. Floating over this newly formed harmonic cushion, there appears a variation of the original tune. I might add that this musical construction is much like the phenomenon known as "fractals"—the geometric language invented by Benoit Mandelbrot to describe "self-similarity" in nature. Mandelbrot made it simple by breaking off a piece from a cauliflower to show that the small piece looks like the whole vegetable in miniature. In the passage by Mozart (and there are many such passages in works by Mozart, Beethoven and other great composers), the melodic "piece" has generated a musical structure with three interconnected self-similar layers. Now it is time for the inevitable question: Did Mozart *know* he was doing this, or are we reading into the music? Was he aware of the layers or simply writing what sounded good to him, without working it out?

To answer this, we must understand that composing (not just tunes but more involved pieces) involves the integration of ideas and form. At best, ideas (substance) and form seem inseparable; they do not merely co-exist in a work, but are a unified entity. This can be understood by thinking again of nature. Living organisms, for example, are both substance and system. We are cells and, getting really small, we are enzymes, proteins and eventually atoms, and these are our substance. This substance is organized into particular patterns (heart, lungs, blood vessels, etc.), forming a system, such as a human being. So, too, in music, there is the substance (motifs, themes, rhythmic gestures) and patterns (harmonic, imitative, repetitive, recapitulatory) that form a system (the piece itself, a sonata, quartet, symphony, opera.) When we reduce a living thing to its measurable parts, we often miss what makes it alive and particular, and its system of patterns and inter-relationships. While it is awe-inspiring to consider that we are made of the same stuff as the stars (as I do in *Music's Deep Physics*), we are not actually stars and stars are not human because of our particular network, our system, our form. To understand a living organism, we measure its substance and map its patterns. To understand a piece of music, we do the same.

Mozart's music (and that of all good and great composers) is not made only of tunes (substance), but also of patterns, relationships and networks. To listen only to basic musical components (tunes, for example), is a kind of reductionism that misses the big picture.

This kind of listener is like a doctor who does not know how his patient lives, whether he smokes, drinks, what he eats or whether he exercises, or even the medical history of his family.

It is the ideas and the patterns together that make great music. The patterns create metaphors that engage our memories. When those metaphors can be grasped, even unconsciously, we perceive the work as meaningful.

I was recently confronted personally with the question of what a composer knows about his own music. A concert presenter invited me to speak to an audience about my second string quartet, *Turning, Returning*, in conjunction with a performance by the Brentano String Quartet. Having given many lectures about *other* composers' works, I felt confident that I could easily talk about my own music without much preparation. The night before the event, I opened the score and stared at the notes. I began to quietly panic, as I realized that I had nothing to say about this piece. Knowing that I had to come up with something by the next day, I decided to examine the piece as if someone else had composed it. With a red pen, I quickly and furiously circled patterns, drew lines connecting related passages, identified variants of ideas and drew a diagram of the work's architecture. To my delight, there was plenty to talk about. But, suddenly, the question hit me as never before: Did I *know* that I was doing that? Considering the speed and ease with which I had just analyzed the work, I concluded that I *did* know all about the piece, but that I had not thought of the techniques as divorced from the *sound* of the piece. I knew the work's patterns, relationships, variants and architecture as music, not as words, not to *speak of.* The next evening, I gave a kind of non-lecture about the piece. Instead of describing and analyzing the music, I told the story of my panic and discovery concerning my own knowledge of the work's design. It became, like this essay, a discussion of what a composer knows, or rather *how* a composer knows his own music.

What did Mozart know? Mozart knew the whole story, imagined his music as a living organism, and created patterns of great elegance and subtlety. He knew every aspect of his music *as* music, in sound, not necessarily in words—the ideas, the relationships, the whole.

# Must It Be?

## (OR MUST IT BE ABOUT?)

DOES KNOWING ABOUT a composer, or about the circumstances of a work, really help us appreciate the music? How does knowing that Beethoven, late in life, flung soup at a waiter, sometimes asked for the bill before ordering his food or refused to pay after a meal, peered frighteningly into people's windows, let his hair and beard grow wild, punned incessantly, demanded control over his nephew Karl against Karl's mother's wishes, attacked his brother, Nikolaus Johann, for living with a woman out of marriage, slept with his friends' wives and patronized prostitutes help us understand, say, the sublime late string quartets?

Certainly, his wild behavior can be heard in the music of the F Minor String Quartet Opus 95, or is it rather Beethoven's more private anxiety over his deafness that is manifest in that violent and mercurial score? But if we knew nothing of Beethoven's life, had no record of his deafness or his battle over his nephew or his failures with women, how then would we hear the violence of Opus 95?

To turn it around, we only *care* about the life of this extraordinary man *because* of the power of the music. We care about the music because it vividly portrays suffering, struggle, triumph, sorrow, rage and humor—not just *his* suffering, *his* struggle, *his* triumph, *his* sorrow, rage and humor. All of it is evident in the music. His life story adds supporting evidence, and occasionally allows, or even encourages, backward appreciation and trivialization, such as hearing his music as proof that a messy person can find order in art, or that a person with a disability (his deafness has been called that in the 1990's) can still be an overachiever.

Certainly, it can be fun to draw parallels between the music and the life. Beethoven's *scherzos*, for example, are full of rude rhythmic and harmonic shocks as well as enharmonic puns (musical *double entendres*), which are consonant with his verbal style in everyday life. But the humor in the music should be enough, *should* it not?

Does knowing *about* the story behind music ever help us understand it in a meaningful way? Perhaps the work most debated in this regard is the finale of Beethoven's last string quartet, Opus 135—the famous *"Muss es sein? Es muss sein!"* movement. It has a real-life behind-the-scenes story that has inspired arguments among musicians, musicologists and even casual music lovers for generations. The story goes that Ignaz Dembscher wanted to borrow the music for Beethoven's quartet Opus 130 for a quartet party at his home. But Dembscher had not attended the premiere of Opus 130, and so Beethoven demanded that Dembscher pay the price of a subscription to the concert, fifty gulders. Dembscher replied, *"Wenn es sein muss!"* (If it has to be). In good humor, with a touch of sarcasm, Beethoven dashed off a canon based on the words *"Es muss sein! Ja, ja, ja, ja! Heraus mit dem Beutel!"* ("It must be! Yes, yes, yes, yes! Hand over your wallet!") If the music based on this were another quirky scherzo, the whole affair would be quite simple. But the resulting music is quite complex, and musical "authorities" (always a suspicious concept) have not agreed whether the finale of Opus 135 is meant to be a comic portrayal of this incident or is, instead, a profound consideration of one of life's great philosophical questions. Beethoven wrote over the top of the last movement: "DER SCHWER GEFASSTE ENTSCHLUSS" ("The hard-made decision"). This is followed by musical settings of the reluctant, brooding question *"Muss es sein?"* ("Must it be?") and the joyous (or is it gloating?) response *"Es muss sein!"* ("It must be!")

In his powerful, moving book, *Beethoven: His Spiritual Development,* J.W.N. Sullivan asserts that even though the "motto had its origin in a joke", it is used in the quartet as "a summary of the great Beethovenian problem of destiny and submission." Sullivan does hear lightness and humor in the music, but he understands it as the humor "of one to whom the issue is settled and familiar." Sullivan concludes: "There is no real conflict depicted in this last movement; the portentous question meets with a jovial, almost exultant answer, and the ending is one of perfect confidence." The British writer Roger Fiske, in his article on Beethoven's chamber music, is sure that this "little" quartet "does not attempt to plumb the depths of human experience, yet achieves something very near perfection in its own humorous epigrammatic way." To Joseph Kerman, whose brilliant book on Beethoven's string quartets is still the principal guide to the works, the development of the *Muss es sein?* motif sounds "more like a farcical depiction of an old miser's discomfiture than any deep serious speculation." Kerman hears the movement as operatic and "parodistic", and suggests that Beethoven may have been mocking his own music, particularly the Ninth Symphony.

Romain Rolland, author of *Jean-Christophe* and of important, romantic works about Beethoven, remarks that Beethoven is a typical German in the way that he turns an ordinary occurrence into a profound philosophical question, all as naturally as breathing. He compares it to a situation in which a servant delivers mustard after the master has eaten. The master says, "too late", and then adds, "as ever in this life", immediately transforming a triviality into a weighty matter. Rolland writes, "...the trivial response evoked the serious question, in an altogether different tone of voice—a question that surged from the very depths of the Beethovenian soul...". If this *had* been a piece inspired by tardy mustard, surely Beethoven, had he spoken English, would have given us "Mustard sein?" instead of "Muss es sein?" A terrible joke—but I have let it stand because it is the kind of nonsensical punning that Beethoven enjoyed. (Must mustard tardy be?)

In his BBC guide to Beethoven's quartets, Basil Lam points out that "no one can disprove" a "highly sophisticated view" that this music may be regarded as "histrionic." But he feels that Beethoven would not "mock at intensity of feeling." After arguing with himself, he concludes, "It is idle to speculate about Beethoven's intentions..." Is it really so hard to tell whether Beethoven is kidding or not? I certainly know people whose sarcasm is both funny and painful, and wasn't

Freud correct in maintaining that all good jokes are funny because they are in some measure true (serious)?

George Bernard Shaw's writings about Beethoven's quartets are the confident assessment of a man of the theater. He hears the middle quartets, which are not often debated and are viewed by most musicians as brilliant, as "intentional intellectualities, profundities, theatrical fits and starts, and wayward caprices of self-conscious genius." Shaw sees the *late* quartets, including our Opus 135, as "beautiful, simple, straightforward, unpretentious, perfectly intelligible." In a review in *The Hornet* in 1894, Shaw complained that the late quartets were not performed often enough: "Are they always avoided because the professors once pronounced them obscure and impossible?"

If Shaw is correct, if the music is "simple" and "straightforward", then perhaps it would do to ask how we would perceive the music if Beethoven had never written the motto at the top, if there were no clue to its meaning at all, and, therefore, no connection to the anecdote that caused all the trouble. That would argue for concert presenters and ensembles to do away with program notes altogether, and to print simply the words "Listen!" at the top of the program.

Shostakovich used to tell a story that can shed some light on this discussion. The story is not about music at all, but about how an artist survives in a repressive regime: The Czar wants his portrait painted and demands that a famous artist be appointed for the task. The artist cannot help but notice that the Czar's left eye is permanently closed, and that the Czar's left leg is bent at the knee, with his foot dangling in mid-air. "The Czar loves truth," thinks the artist, and so he paints him as he is. When the Czar sees the painting, he is outraged, and the artist is banished to Siberia. Another artist is brought in. He knows that the first artist failed, and so he paints the Czar with both eyes open and both legs planted firmly on the ground. He is also sent to Siberia. A third artist is hired. This artist, Shostakovich tells us, is a survivor, a *yurodovy*, or "jester", who knows how to lie and tell the truth simultaneously. What does he do? He paints the Czar as a hunter in the forest with bow and arrow: his left eye closed as he aims, and his left leg firm upon a rock.

Now the question is: How would we see this painting if we did not know about the Czar's closed eye and lame leg? We could never guess from the painting, alone, that the artist is wickedly clever, nor would we feel the strange balance of comedy and terror that this story reveals. But a painting could be humorous and terrifying in and of itself. Its textures, colors, atmosphere should speak for themselves, no? But if there were such a story told about a mediocre painting, would we care? And what if the story were told about a great painting, and then it turned out that the story was not true?

Hamlet asks a similar question to "Muss es sein?", when Shakespeare has him say, "To be or not to be?" Hamlet is alone when he ponders suicide, so he must be serious about it, right? But perhaps, as some directors have thought, Hamlet suspects that he is being watched. Was Hamlet mad or only pretending? Hamlet says clearly that he will "put an antic disposition on", to *pretend* madness in order to have his way, to be free to behave strangely in order to catch the King.

Yet some directors and actors have decided that he becomes truly mad in the course of the play. Others have concluded that Hamlet says that he will feign madness in order to cover up for his *actual* madness! Muss es sein?

The question underlying this essay is: What do we need to know to appreciate great music? More important than knowing stories *about* the music, is to know more *music*, and to know more about the nature of music itself. Music is a way of understanding the world. The music lover's job is to listen with a willing ear, a curious mind and ready emotions. While music cannot be specific about ordinary things—for example, it cannot give us a recipe for a chocolate cake—music *can* be as sensual as the deepest, darkest chocolate cake of your wildest dreams.

Was Beethoven mocking Ignaz Dembscher's reluctance to pay fifty gulders in the finale to Opus 135 or asking one of life's great questions? Was Hamlet mad, pretending to be mad, or pretending to be pretending to be mad?

As a composer, Beethoven understood that, as W.S. Gilbert wrote, "things are seldom what they seem." Beethoven, in a letter, wrote a few comments about the nature of knowing:

"Let us begin with the primary original causes of all things, how something came about, wherefore and why it came about in that particular way and became what it is, why something is what it is, why something cannot be exactly so!!! Here, dear friend, we have reached the ticklish point, which my delicacy forbids me to reveal to you at once. All that we can say is: *it cannot be.*"

This rambling, seemingly convoluted commentary by the composer could be interpreted as a solution to our riddle of the *Muss es sein?* movement of Opus 135. Let us imagine that the phrases "the primary original causes" and "how something came about" refer to the incident with Ignaz Dembscher. Then we may understand the phrase "became what it is" to mean the composition of the music inspired by that event. We are left with the opinion that "something cannot be exactly so" and that, simply, "it cannot be". Plainly put, something is gained in the translation of a trivial incident into a work of art, something more, something new, something else. We may insist that the music mean only one thing, have one interpretation, that "it must be" so. But, as the composer, himself, said, "It cannot be."

# Chaos and Order:

## COYOTE, SAM SHEPARD AND BEETHOVEN

THE ACT OF COMPOSING BRINGS INTO BALANCE intuition and intellect, emotions and reason, energy and boundaries, play and work, improvisation and organization, freedom and discipline, chaos and order. At some level, all artistic expression is about this balance. This makes sense, since it is also fundamental to our everyday lives: Our need for love and sex finds organized expression in the various rituals of relationships and laws of marriage; our instincts to band together to protect our turf and compete for survival find organized, formal expression in team sports. Competitive sports invariably involve many rules. Rules are the obstacles that define achievement and create the metaphors of the game.

In science, recent work in chaos theory, developed from the pioneering ideas of Jules Henri Poincaré, has shown that seemingly chaotic behavior may, if we investigate, reveal deep-order patterns. Scientists now distinguish between *random* behavior and *chaotic* behavior. With his "fractal" geometry, Benoit Mandelbrot has given mathematicians a way to describe chaotic structures—a language, as he put it, "to speak of clouds, of mountains, of rivers, of lightning." The very goal of science is to bring order to our "chaotic" world by searching for rules that can predict, systems that can explain, just as religion has provided rules and answers to ward off chaos and meaninglessness. The very concept of a split between emotion and reason has been shown by Antonio R. Damasio to be a false premise. Damasio has shown that reason and emotion do not exist separately in the brain, and that no apparently objective or rational decision can really be devoid of emotional quality. (See his book *Descartes' Error: Emotion and Reason in the Human Brain*.)

I would like to present three provocative artistic manifestations of the struggle between order and chaos, reason and emotion: an archetypal Native American creation myth; a play by Sam Shepard; and a string quartet by Ludwig van Beethoven. My main goal is to illuminate the fundamental issues of the *Grosse Fuge* of Beethoven, often perceived as one of the most difficult compositions to understand in the history of music, in terms of a struggle as ancient as an Indian myth and as modern as a Sam Shepard play. The Indian story will be presented separately, since it states the conflict in pure terms. The Sam Shepard play and the Beethoven quartet are then presented in counterpoint.

## COYOTE SCATTERS THE STARS
### (based on versions from several Southwestern tribes )

One day, a very long time ago, before there were stars in the sky, Great Grandmother Spirit gave a large jar full of shining stars to First Man. She also gave him a thick book that showed in great detail where the stars should go in the sky. Great Grandmother told First Man to place the stars in the sky very carefully, according to the book, and not to deviate from the designs contained in the book in any way.

Slowly and methodically, First Man began placing the stars in the sky. He consulted the charts in the book every few moments. He would look at the sky, then at a chart and only when he was absolutely sure that he would get it right, First Man stuck a star firmly in its appointed place in the enormous sky. Every now and then, he stopped and compared the sky to the appropriate chart, and felt proud.

After much time had passed in this way, Coyote happened along. He watched First Man for a few minutes, then asked, "What are you doing there?"

"Don't you see," answered First Man, "I'm putting the stars in the sky according to this book. The charts in this book represent the plan as conceived by Great Grandmother Spirit."

"Uh huh," mused Coyote, not as impressed as most of us would be. Coyote watched for a few more moments, but soon he grew impatient, which, if you know Coyote, is typical.

"You're so slow!" yapped Coyote.

"But it must be done exactly right!" First Man explained. "If I rush it might get messy." "Big deal! Who cares about that stupid book, anyway!" Coyote howled. "Just throw the stars up there, and let them stick where they want!"

"No!" shouted First Man, shocked at Coyote's attitude. "Give me that jar!" yelped Coyote. "I'll throw the stars way up there! It'll be done much faster, and it'll look spectacular!"

First Man clutched the jar of stars to his chest and cautioned Coyote, "It's all organized perfectly in the book! Your way would be total chaos, you crazy Coyote!"

At this point, unable to contain himself (and annoyed at being called "crazy"), Coyote grabbed at the jar. But First Man held on tight with both hands, keeping the book squeezed under one arm. They wrestled this way for a long time.

Suddenly, First Man's grip gave way, the book hit the dirt, and Coyote, holding on to the jar of stars, flipped over backwards from the force of his own yanking. Coyote jumped up and began dancing about wildly, foreshadowing the work of Martha Graham by an eternity. Then Coyote triumphantly opened the jar, tossed the lid over his shoulder, and, with one paw in the jar, stood there leering at First Man.

"Watch this, Mr. Organized !" laughed Coyote, scattering the stars all about the heavens, throwing some straight up above his head, others to the right, some to the left, flicking some of them Frisbee-style into the void.

He growled with delight, and called back over his shoulder to First Man,

"*You* call it chaos, *I* call it Beauty!"

And even to this very day (or night, rather), if you look at the sky, you will see that some stars look very orderly and evenly spaced, while others are bunched up in a mess or twinkling off in a corner alone. We can still see First Man's carefully placed stars, reflecting Great Grandmother Spirit's design, as well as the randomly thrown stars flung by Coyote.

# CHAOS AND ORDER

## Sam Shepard's *True West* and
## Beethoven's *Grosse Fuge, Opus 133*

In "True West", two brothers — one a wild outlaw (Lee), the other a disciplined, conventional Ivy League graduate (Austin) — are locked in a struggle throughout the play. Austin, at his mother's home while she is away, is busy writing a screenplay, and has a producer, Saul Kimmer, interested in his work. Lee, who has been living aimlessly in the desert, barges in on his brother. Drunk and confrontational, Lee not only disturbs Austin's work, but also soon convinces Saul Kimmer to produce a movie based on his true story as a wild nomad in the west instead of Austin's screenplay. Austin now is forced to collaborate with Lee, which means he has to write the script for him. In a wonderfully ironic speech, Austin compares himself to Lee and simultaneously states an idea central to the main conflict:

"He's been camped out in the desert for three months. Talking to cactus. What's he know about what people wann' see on the screen! I drive on the freeway every day. I swallow the smog. I watch the news in color. I shop in the Safeway. I'm the one who's in touch! Not him!"

Soon, it is Lee who has buckled down to work and Austin who has become a wild drunk. The brothers switch roles. Each might have been the other. Metaphorically, they are two aspects of a single, more integrated human being. This idea is articulated in the script itself:

Austin: You're going to write an entire script on your own?

Lee: That's right.

Austin: Here's a thought. Saul Kimmer——

Lee: Shut up will ya'!

Austin: He thinks we're the same person.

Lee: Don't get cute.

Austin: He does! He's lost his mind. Poor old Saul. Thinks we're one in the same.

The brothers go on to destroy their mother's house and nearly kill each other. The play ends with the brothers squared off, watching each other like two animals in a fight to the death.

The struggle between Lee (real life, chaos) and Austin (art, order) is also symbolized powerfully in this play by the continuous background presence of coyotes. The coyote, just as in the Indian myth related above, is used by Shepard to suggest the constant threat of chaos. In his note on the sound to be used throughout the production of *True West*, Shepard writes:

"The Coyote of Southern California has a distinct yapping, dog-like bark, similar to a Hyena. This yapping grows more intense and maniacal as the pack grows in numbers, which is usually the case when they lure and kill pets from suburban yards. The sense of growing frenzy in the pack should be felt in the background, particularly in scenes 7 and 8. In any case, these Coyotes never make the long mournful, solitary howl of the Hollywood stereotype."

Earlier in the play, at the very end of Act I, Lee describes to Austin a scene in his imagined movie, drawn from life. The speech is a perfect summary of the two brothers themselves, their struggle and fate:

"So they take off after each other straight into an endless black prairie. The sun is just comin' down and they can feel the night on their backs. What they don't know is that each one of 'em is afraid, see, each one separately thinks that he's the only one that's afraid. And they keep ridin' like that straight into the night. Not knowing. And the one who's chasin' doesn't know where the other one is taking him. And the one who's being chased doesn't know where he's going."

This speech also wonderfully describes the frightening chase that is Beethoven's *Grosse Fuge*. The word fugue is derived from *fuir*, to flee (like fugitive). Traditionally, each voice enters and states the "*subject*" (or main idea) and then "flees" in a "countersubject" while the next voice enters. In medicine, a *fugue* is a condition of mental confusion in which a patient feels that he has fled his body, that he is outside (or beside) himself. Both of these concepts of *fugue* relate to the central theme of *True West*.

Beethoven gave us a clue to the meaning of this work at the top of the manuscript. Above the music, he inscribed: "*Tantôt libre, tantôt recherchée*" ("at times natural/free, at times learned/disciplined"), suggesting a conflict similar to that of Lee (*libre*) and Austin (*recherchée*). Beethoven was himself struggling with a fundamental artistic dichotomy, the weight of a great technical tradition (fugue) and the unbound energy of his imagination. Put simply, it is the struggle of form and content, which, in a great work, must be organically bound together. In the *Grosse Fuge*, however, Beethoven has consciously set form and content against each other in a kind of contest of power. It is a unique moment in the history of musical thinking. The work's maniacal power comes from a relentless double fugue, whose two subjects collide with each other with fierce energy. The fact that it is a *double* fugue further intensifies the sense of confrontation between ideas and the composer's battle to capture them in form.

In *True West*, it is possible to view Lee as *content* (the man of real experience with a story worth telling) and Austin as *form* (a literate, educated and disciplined writer in search of a story). At the play's end, the struggle continues as the lights dim. In the quartet, there is a clear sense of triumph. Beethoven conquers chaos; the artist-hero prevails.

More than Lee and more than Austin (who are aspects of one person), Beethoven was an outrageously wild man and also a disciplined, uncompromisingly self-critical worker. He seemed to have had a keen understanding of the search for the balance between unbound freedom of imagination and the power of constraint inherent in musical expression. Beethoven suffered the agonies of deafness and of utter failure in love. He lived in a desert of isolation, physical and sexual. He yearned for the simplicity of his brother's family life. He fought insanely to become the legal guardian of his orphaned nephew against the will of his brother's widow, and later the nephew attempted suicide. This was a man full of rage. Music both restrained and released his rage. Beethoven let his wordless rage explode like a Big Bang, into this *Great Fugue*. The *Grosse Fuge* is a desperate chase across the landscape of his emotions and reason. It is uncompromising, unashamed and fearless. This work has its own severe laws and particular chaos, its own prisons and escapes.

I will not attempt to describe the *Grosse Fuge*, but rather urge you to listen to it, and to read Shepard's *True West* (or rent the video.) The best I can do here is to bounce metaphors from one work to the next, in hopes that they will collide, generating archetypal revelations of great force.

A final thought: Leonard Bernstein conjured up Beethoven's *Great Fugue* in *West Side Story* at just the right moment in the drama. The gang called the Jets is getting ready to "rumble" with the Sharks. They feel terrified and excited, ready to fight. In the song "Cool", they try to reign in their violent urges, to wait until the right moment, to play it cool. During the dance that is the main segment of this scene, Bernstein paraphrases the *Grosse Fuge* in a mock fugue (which he labels "Fugue"). It is a perfect use of the music. He hardly needs to alter the *Grosse Fuge*, so modern is its urgency and timeless is its struggle: "Go man, go, but not like a yo-yo schoolboy! Just play it cool, boy. Real cool."

# Brahms and the Man:

## George Bernard Shaw and Johannes Brahms

THE GREAT PLAYWRIGHT GEORGE BERNARD SHAW was also a music critic who found many occasions to attack the music of Brahms. In an article written June 24, 1891, Shaw wrote:

"The admirers of Brahms had a succulent treat at the Richter concert last week. His German Requiem was done from end to end, and done quite well enough to bring out all its qualities. What those qualities are could have been guessed by a deaf man from the mountainous tedium of the unfortunate audience, who yet listened with a perverse belief that Brahms is a great composer, and the performance of this masterpiece of his an infinitely solemn and important function. I am afraid that this delusion was not confined to those who, having found by experience that good music bores them, have rashly concluded that all music that bores them must be good. It raged also among the learned musicians, who know what a *point d'orgue* is, and are delighted to be able to explain what is happening when Brahms sets a pedal pipe booming and a drum thumping the dominant of the key for *ten minutes* at a stretch, whilst the other instruments and the voices plow along through every practicable progression in or near the key, up hill from syncopation to syncopation, and down dale from suspension to suspension in an elaborately modernized manner that only makes the whole operation seem more desperately old-fashioned and empty."

The pedal point on the dominant to which Shaw refers does not really last ten minutes. On a recording of the *Requiem* as performed by the Atlanta Symphony conducted by Robert Shaw (no relation), the pedal point lasts only three minutes. The New York Philharmonic as conducted by Kurt Masur plays the same passage in two minutes. (Brahms would not have minded the discrepancies. He hated the metronome and its implication that there was a single correct  tempo for any music. He refused to indicate "mechanical" markings for his *Requiem*.)  But however long the pedal point may be,  far more important is Shaw's attack on Brahms's use of *point d'orgue* at all (and on those "learned musicians" who are "delighted to be able to explain what is happening"....I suppose that would be me.)

A *point d'orgue*—which Shaw could just as well have called by its English name "organ point" or, more commonly, "pedal point"—is a sustained tone (or tones) around which other voices move.  Its name is derived from the foot pedals on the organ. An organist can plant a foot on a deep-voiced pedal note and simply leave it there while keeping his hands busy about the keyboards, shifting harmonies above.

Shaw, the irritated critic, continued:

"Brahms seems to have been impressed by the fact that Beethoven produced remarkable effects by persisting with his pedal points long after Mozart would have resolved them, and to have convinced himself by an obvious logical process that it must be possible to produce still more remarkable results by outdoing Beethoven in persistency."

Soon Shaw reveals that it is not merely the duration of Brahms's pedal points that annoys him, but the fact that he uses them at all:

"The fact is, there is nothing a genuine musician regards with more jealousy than an attempt to pass off the forms of music for music itself, especially those forms which have received a sort of consecration from their use by great composers in the past."

He accuses Brahms *and* those who like his "empty" forms of thinking "that it is the cowl that makes the monk." In 1893, writing about Brahms's chamber music, Shaw again takes a stab at pedal points: "To me it seems quite obvious that the real Brahms is nothing more than a sentimental voluptuary with a wonderful ear. For respectability's sake he adopts the forms academically supposed to be proper to great composers, since it gives him no trouble to pile up *points d'orgue*, as in the *Requiem...*"

For his part, Brahms really adored pedal points. They are everywhere in his music. The D Minor Violin Sonata has a rather enormous one in the first movement, lasting the entire development section. In his Piano Quartet in C Minor—in which his anxiety over his love for Clara Schumann, the wife of his mentor, Robert Schumann, is given full reign — Brahms uses pedal points to powerful effect. Virtually every work of Brahms boasts a footful of pedals. The question is, why did Shaw attack the very concept of the pedal point, and why did Brahms use it so often?

To get to the heart of the controversy, one must ask, "What does a pedal point *mean*?" Musical devices, forms, techniques that have endurance, have meaning. They convey, metaphorically, an aspect of what — for lack of a better expression—we call *real life*. A pedal point is a constant, a persistent, fixed tone in the presence of other, active music. It may suggest something unalterable, or inevitable, or inexorable, something that is always *there* — like God, death, taxes. To update the metaphor, we might think of contemporary pedal points such as Barnes and Noble, Starbucks, McDonald's, the Gap, Banana Republic and Border's. Found in every city and village, these stores are common commercial pedal points that provide a constant background to the counterpoint of daily life. In a grander view, the pedal point might suggest a power, be it church or state, or it might convey the idea of love, a great, undying devotion— spiritual or sensual.

Let's examine Shaw and Brahms with respect to the metaphorical view of pedal points.

A true iconoclast and free thinker, George Bernard Shaw had little use for anything established and powerful. He certainly did not care for the church or the state. A typical comment about the state from this famous Fabian Socialist proves the point: "The established government of England has no more right to call itself the state than the smoke of London has to call itself the weather." Of the church, Shaw wrote, "It is as easy for me to believe that the universe made itself as that a maker of the universe made himself, in fact much easier; for the universe visibly exists and makes itself as it goes along, whereas a maker for it is a hypothesis." Although Shaw would not speak against love, he had a low regard for the institution of marriage. The middle-aged Shaw married his friend Charlotte Payne-Townsend, because he saw, as he put it, "no other solution." A friend, who had come to nurse him after a physical collapse from overwork, Payne-Townsend agreed to an unromantic union. On their honeymoon, Shaw wrote the book *The Perfect Wagnerite.* (Certainly not *The Ideal Husband.*)

Johannes Brahms, like Shaw, was not particularly religious, though a profoundly spiritual person. Brahms removed from the *Requiem* text the reference to Jesus in order to make it a *Requiem* for all humanity. He called the work *A German Requiem*, not *The* German Requiem, and he stated that it should perhaps best be called *A Human Requiem.* Unlike Shaw, he was not a revolutionary or political animal. But that he felt the pull of conventional religion to some extent is clear from the fact that he composed a requiem at all. And the music does convey profound ties to the history of religious compositions, including the powerful metaphor of the pedal point. Brahms was no iconoclast. He revered not only Beethoven and Schubert, but also masters of the more distant past, including Handel, Couperin, Palestrina and, most importantly, Johann Sebastian Bach.

As for love, Brahms fell into it often. First in importance among his loves, throughout his life, was Clara Schumann, the pianist-composer, and wife of Brahms's great friend and mentor, Robert Schumann. When Robert Schumann suffered from mental illness and was sent away for a time, Brahms helped Clara take care of her seven children. It was during this period, when Brahms was in his early twenties, that he began composing his emotionally charged Piano Quartet in C Minor, a work he could not bring himself to complete to his satisfaction until nearly twenty years later. Brahms never married.

Shaw married without romantic love, and Brahms loved romantically without marriage. Perhaps this can shed some light on the pedal point dispute. Was Clara Schumann the living *point d'orgue* of Brahms? Could Shaw, who had rejected the certainties of church and state as well as the inexorable power of romantic love, possibly find meaning in a pedal point?

There is a series of letters between Clara and Johannes that illuminate this question most remarkably. Brahms wrote to Clara on July 2, 1893: "In a dozen measures, I imagine I can see you smile a bit (which ones?)." Clara wrote back to him less than a week later: "I think I'll be able to find the dozen measures that you mention." Two weeks later, Johannes wrote to Clara: "*The pedal point...is, of course, the passage where I have been counting on your happy face. I know your old weakness for pedal points.*"

So it is about love, after all. Whether or not it was the pedal point's metaphorical power to suggest enduring love (and so Clara adored it), or just Brahms's desire to secretly thrill Clara by using a technique she enjoyed, is unknowable. Perhaps both Brahms and Clara Schumann loved the pedal point for its historical resonance, its Bachian majesty. Perhaps they felt, but never consciously articulated, the pedal point's significance as a metaphor for their own relationship: a constant bond that could never be publicly acknowledged; a spiritual and intellectual kinship that underscored a three-part counterpoint, which included Robert Schumann. (This could also explain Brahms's obsession with the polyrhythm of three-beats against two.)

Perhaps in some unconscious way, Shaw was irritated by the meaning of the metaphor, and *not*, as he thought, by its *lack* of meaning in Brahms's music. In the end, it is very personal indeed.

Shaw eventually changed his mind about Brahms. He apologized to his readers in 1936 for misunderstanding the music of Brahms, who died in 1897:

"In every composer's work there are passages that are part of the common stock of music of the time; and when a new genius arises, and his idiom is still unfamiliar and, therefore, even disagreeable, it is easy for a critic who knows that stock to recognize its contributions to the new work and fail to take in the original complexion put upon it. Beethoven denounced Weber's Euryanthe overture as a string of diminished sevenths. I had not yet got hold of the idiosyncratic Brahms. I apologize."

The long pedal point of a tirade was finally resolved.

# DETACHMENT AND PERFECTION

## TRANCES, CRAFT AND MAURICE RAVEL

LEONARD BERNSTEIN SAID IN A WELL-KNOWN INTERVIEW that musical ideas "seize" him, that he felt himself "a slave" of the creative act, and that this glorious state of creative thought cannot be consciously induced. He admitted that there are many methods that might bring about the "loss of ego" necessary to receive ideas – including yoga, meditation, peyote (!), and self-imposed trances — but that nothing would "guarantee that that's going to turn out F sharps." The creative trance, which I have described in the essay *Music's Deep Physics*, is only half the process. The ability to catch and retain those inspired ideas in order to work with them, to mold them into coherent musical forms, is commonly called "technique". The dizzy buzz of inspiration is ecstatic and emotionally vivid, but the selection of ideas and the act of constructing a piece require patience and clear-headedness. Both the trance and the working-out stages of creativity (the famous "inspiration and perspiration") have a curious detachment. Bernstein's professed "loss of ego" and my term "vanishing" are meant to convey the feeling of being in the audience of your own mind. That level of detachment (trance) is quite different from the clear head that is necessary in the working-out stage. Here the composer is not in the audience but is, rather, like the house manager in the theater. The manager knows all the rules and procedures, keeps order, and neither performs nor applauds.

Not every composer would agree with this description of the creative act. There are those who discover ideas only after having begun a technical process. For them, the craft itself is also the inspiration. Most composers know what it means to work in both conditions: from the inspired moment to the desk, and from the desk to the inspired moment. In either case, when a composer is a master craftsman, musicians and audiences can feel it. In the music of some composers, we can also hear the detachment. There is an emotional distance, a kind of sublimation of passion to reason, which is evident in the work of many fine composers. Often, the emotional distance is an aspect of the composer's aesthetic. It is Apollonian rather than Dionysian.

Maurice Ravel's work embodies a high degree of Apollonian detachment and perfection of craft. Ravel's work habits and musical style were a perfect reflection of the way he lived his life. The detachment, which may also be heard as elegance, was typical of Ravel, the man.

Maurice Ravel was a collector of fine items, musical and otherwise. Perfect contraptions, like his toy nightingale that flapped and sang, or his miniature mechanical sale boat that rocked in a paper sea, inspired a music that twirls, that spins its melodies above a porcelain harmony. He dipped his pen into a favorite cathedral-shaped inkwell, the closest he got to conventional theology. Then, like a thief planning a complex museum heist, he charted the details of his very private music. Music so private, that one wonders whether he hid some of his passions from himself.

"I don't have ideas," he told a friend. Instead, he played "connect-the-dots" with his still wet notes, drawing conclusions from random musings, like a painter whose brush seems to know what he will do next. "I don't know what I think 'til I hear what I say," says an Oscar Wilde character. "It was a dark and stormy night," Snoopy types, as he sits on his doghouse, and then wonders what on earth the next sentence might be.

Discovering his thoughts in the act of writing, Ravel refused to admit to any mystery; he thought himself to be a patient chiseler. Ravel insisted that his craft was more method than muse, perhaps because he was afraid of something inside himself, perhaps as protection from the glare of his own brilliance. He declared that composing was seventy-five percent an intellectual endeavor, that the notion of inspired ideas was trivial. He didn't believe in bolts of inspiration, nor impassioned sketching, trying to catch the moment. The inspiration comes with the working out. To do is all. To work — but not from theories! "All theory is gray," Ravel noted, "but the precious tree of life is green." He was also fond of saying, with Baudelaire, "Inspiration is merely the reward for working every day."

We cannot ever really know if he burned inside like Janáček or Beethoven. He said that he did not — and certainly his music is not so much "fire" itself, but rather its vivid reflection caught perfectly in a windowpane. Yet, like Janáček and Messiaen, he knew the songs of many birds, could whistle their tunes, and carefully observed the markings of plants and the activities of insects. If he believed in any kind of god, he knew to find him in the details.

Driving a truck near Verdun during the First World War, Ravel found himself in the midst of the terrifying clamor of battle, followed by the most unearthly stillness. At dawn, the hush was broken by the sudden song of a warbler. Ravel was moved, captivated. Although he never wrote it, he declared his intention to write a song to be called "The Unconcerned Warbler". The title is revealing. Might not Janáček have heard a message of peace in the warbler's melody, or a song of thanks that the battle had ended, or a lonely cry for a mate? Would Messiaen have heard the bird's song as a message from God that love will rule in the end? That Ravel heard the bird's song as "unconcerned", and that this "unconcern" appealed to him, speaks volumes. Did Ravel see himself as that warbler, able to bring a detached beauty into the frightening, dangerous world?

Perhaps, Ravel was right about the warbler. Perhaps, any other interpretation of the bird's song would be a romanticization, a falsification. In any case, Ravel understood that beauty stands apart from the noise of politics, aloof from madness of power and the screams of history.

Dressing well was his best revenge. Ravel's collection of toys and miniatures was almost matched by his array of ties and jackets. Whether or not he was an unconcerned warbler, Ravel seemed a peacock to his friends. A bit of a dandy (but never to be confused with the composer D'Indy), Ravel knew how to cloak a melody in silken textures, how to spread a chord across an ensemble like a cape over the shoulder, how to place perfectly rows of pizzicato pitches like so many shiny buttons on a splendid coat. There is never a loose thread in a piece by Ravel, everything fits, tailored to perfection. If the seams sometimes show, they are splendidly pressed.

Just as a label in a jacket these days may boast the name of a French designer and say made in Korea, there are signs in some of Ravel's music pointing to his models, those composers whose work he admired and even imitated. Ravel saw no shame in imitation. He told his close friends on many occasions, "If you have nothing to say, you cannot do better, while waiting for the ultimate silence, than repeat what has been well said. If you do have something to say, that something will never be more clearly seen than in your unwitting infidelity to the model." From Debussy he learned how to use sensuous, complex harmonies, exotic modes and floating progressions. Ravel used these riches lovingly, and with Mozartian economy. Also an advocate of musical economy, Stravinsky commented that one should treat intervals like dollars. He even tried to advise Ravel on real-life financial matters, for which Ravel had no head at all. Ravel, at least, treated his notes like francs, each measure a "bar" of gold.

It may be that Ravel's Mozartian economy and elegance, his taste for classical balance, saved him, in part, from being a Debussy clone. Debussy, like a musician from the Orient, could love a sound for its lonely beauty, but Ravel had to know its purpose, its place in the harmonic progression. Ravel borrowed the extended harmonic vocabulary of Debussy, but not Debussy's revolutionary methods. Debussy loved mystery; Ravel preferred magic tricks. Debussy, the mystic poet. Ravel, the sorcerer. Debussy insisted, "Pleasure is the law." Ravel might have said, "There is pleasure in the law." Debussy was a true revolutionary, who stripped the clothes off music. Natural, unreasonable, playful, impolite, Debussy's music is vulnerable, risky. Ravel dressed his music in the finest French and exotic fabrics, the latest fashions, with expert makeup, perfect lighting. Ravel had no interest in artistic revolution. He compared revolution to breaking a window with a rock to get fresh air. "I have no need to break the window. I know how to open it," he remarked.

But after Debussy died in 1918, Ravel broke some windows. In his compositions of the 1920's, Ravel experimented with Germanic dissonance (of an almost Schoenbergian bite), jazz-inspired music and polytonality (music simultaneously in more than one tonality). In his pieces *Chansons Madécasses* (1925-26), the *Sonata for Violin and Cello*, and the *Sonata for Violin and Piano*, Ravel unleashed new energy, taking him far away from the world of Debussy. But daring as Ravel may have been, the music never has the quality of experimentation; it is always perfect in technique, controlled in expression, detached.

Contrary to Ravel's own assertions, I have to believe that the composer, perhaps unaware, was now and then caught up in inspired trances and musical dreams. Ravel loved to be alone with his collection of mechanical toys, knick-knacks and glass baubles. His piano was covered with them. He must have loved to hear them whir and buzz, to watch them glint and glisten in the sunlight that streamed in through the window. Perhaps it was this that inspired Ravel to create so many delicate, transparent, spinning melodies, which gleam and shimmer in the sharply focused light of his ever-shifting, intricate harmonies.

# Innovation or Renovation:
## Postmodernism is Nothing New

*".. time future contained in time past.."* T.S. Eliot

When we talk of creative genius, we tend to emphasize innovation, originality, novelty and revolution. But this tendency obscures an important and enduring facet of the creative process: returning to the past to discover the future. "Postmodernism", contrary to the assertions of near-sighted critics, is neither a new phenomenon nor unique to our time. In every age, artists have embraced and incorporated historical concepts and techniques, even of the distant past. The spirit of deliberate archaism common today has existed for centuries. Composers, especially the most "original" and influential, have studied the great music of their predecessors, utilized ancient techniques and traditions, and, in doing so, have revealed their own personalities all the more. (The term postmodernism seems to mean one thing to musicologists, another to literary threorists and nothing at all to many composers, including George Rochberg and Ned Rorem who have publicly ridiculed the concept.)

The sensibility of discovery through the past in music parallels the formation of a mature, individual personality in life. We hope to grow wiser with experience —but what does that mean? It means that we gather memories, and memory forms the basis for our ability to assess new experiences, to ascertain meaning. As this network of memories expands, so does our ability to cross-reference, reflect, understand and predict. Our intuition becomes more reliable. Our past is with us always, not in the form of finished scenes ready for reference, but in evolving images unconsciously transformed by present experience. Just as it is a mistake to reduce the development of a human being's personality to a linear series of events or to assume that we naturally learn (and should be taught) sequentially, so, too, it is an unhelpful simplification to view music history as a linear progression of styles. We can only view our past in the light of our present. Musically, we define what is enduring—or, to a composer, *useful*—from the past in the context of our present musical diction. That which endures has authenticity, truth. Musical forms and procedures that ring true may fall out of fashion, but they are bound to reappear.

What we usually call our "cultural heritage" might well be thought of as our cultural memory — not an unconscious collective memory, but a tangible, available body of work. This concept personalizes the past, which is exactly what creative artists do. Studying, copying and incorporating the music of the past builds the network of memory and experience.

Bach, whose work greatly expanded the emotional and technical dimensions of the art of music, had a vast knowledge of the music of other composers, contemporary and ancient. In a tradition similar to the emulation of masters in

the visual arts, Bach transcribed and parodied other composer's music, revealing new aspects of their music in the process.
Bach's interest in the musical past included the works of
Palestrina and Lotti. He learned from everyone: Vivaldi,
Frescobaldi, Buxtehude, Handel, Telemann and many others.
His music was up-to-date as well as steeped in tradition. An
appreciation of the harmonic and melodic richness, complexity, elegance and power of Bach's counterpoint is further
deepened by an awareness of how he integrates, expands and
enriches the contrapuntal styles of the previous three hundred
years. His music is like an ocean into which all the rivers flow.
It combines the ancient with the new, integrating horizontal
(melodic) and vertical (harmonic) concepts of musical
processes, yielding an unprecedented level of coherence and
balance. Bach unified a multiplicity of historical techniques
and conditions, creating the enduring impression that it is
not merely *his* personal vision of music, but a defining
moment of the art itself. In fact, Bach's music is both deeply
personal and, through its unifying eclecticism, comprehen-
sive and universal. After his death, Bach's work fell into
neglect. Upon its rediscovery, championed by Felix
Mendelssohn, Bach's music became the critical point of reference for generations of composers who looked to the past to
discover *their* present.

Beethoven, in his late works, was also a great unifier of
past and present traditions. His most innovative works, such
as the final string quartets and piano sonatas, owe their pecu-
liar power in great measure to a new historical awareness.
Here is real post-modernism, if we rightly understand the

music of Haydn and Mozart to represent the then-modern style. Finding the linear, narrative scenarios of the classical style limiting and frustrating, Beethoven returned to forgotten or neglected textures and procedures to give expression to passions too far-ranging for current fashion. Turning to fugues, the Bach-inspired concept of chorale prelude (in the *Heiliger Dankgesang* of Opus 132) and brief Baroque-like dance movements (Opus 130), Beethoven saw the history of music as his personal inheritance.

Beethoven transformed the chorale-prelude concept in the *Heiliger Dankgesang* ("Holy Song of Thanksgiving") by presenting it in three self-contained statements, the second and third gaining in emotional intensity as they transform the Baroque texture through fragmentation and feverish dissociation. The three statements are separated by two  pillars of utterly ecstatic music (marked *Neue Kraft* or "New Strength"). This music also becomes more intense in its second incarnation, but by the most elaborate Baroque-inspired ornamentation ever penned. The movement is, therefore, constructed as two independent pieces — the *Heiliger Dankgesang* chorale prelude and the *Neue Kraft* — which are cross-cut, as in cinema technique. The two "scenes" evolve independently but create a powerful single scenario that strengthens both. Thus Beethoven manages to retain the identity and integrity of the old tradition while simultaneously transfiguring and transcending it.

Mendelssohn and Schumann added keyboard accompaniments to solo violin works of Bach, in the belief that Bach's inspiring "studies" for violin could be brought to the concert stage by "the greater richness of means of recent times", as Schumann put it. Schumann's fascination with Bach's ability to imply several voices of counterpoint with a single melody can be heard in the elusive, dreamlike polyphony of Schumann's own piano writing.

Schumann's collection of historical musical manuscripts made a great impression on the young Johannes Brahms. Brahms, too, became an important collector of old manuscripts. In addition to being a composer, Brahms was an editor and avid musicologist whose views on Bach and Mozart were well known. In his lifetime, the first complete editions of the works of Bach, Handel, Lassus, Schütz, Couperin and Palestrina appeared in print. Brahms participated in this revolution of musical scholarship, editing works of Couperin and realizing continuo parts (writing out keyboard parts from shorthand) for some works in the complete Handel edition. Inspired by his study of Bach's chorale settings, Brahms then dug further into the past, examining Lutheran chorales of the Renaissance. In the great tradition of learning by copying out masterworks (a valuable technique of deep learning, uniting mental and physical networking, lost to photocopying), Brahms copied Palestrina's *Missa Pape Marcelli.* He continued in the tradition of Mendelssohn, conducting works long forgotten before a bewildered Viennese audience. His knowledge of the past profoundly informed his own composing. Old forms and procedures—passacaglia, fugue, chorales and elaborate contrapuntal textures unpopular in his own day—appear throughout his work. His E Minor Cello Sonata, Op. 38, pays tribute to Bach, most obviously in the theme of the finale, which is almost a quote of Contrapunctus 13 from Bach's *Art of the Fugue*. Brahms was also captivated by Bach's Chaconne for unaccompanied violin, which he arranged for piano, left hand only, for Clara Schumann.  Employing old forms in his work, Brahms explored a profoundly personal and rich harmonic language. But even in his progressive harmony (as Schoenberg described it), there is an underlying historical sensitivity, especially an interest in archaic modes. The musically trained listener will pick this up in the frequent use of plagal cadences (conjuring up an ancient ecclesiastic tradition), extensive pedals and picardy thirds, among other devices; the untrained listener, if familiar with early music at all, will surely detect the resonance of history.

Debussy expanded music's vocabulary and syntax. He gave a new spin to familiar chords, divorcing them from their traditional functions, creating a floating world without polarity or gravity. Inspired by Javanese, Japanese and Chinese music, Debussy profoundly changed the texture of European music. Yet, this truly revolutionary composer—who said, "There is no theory. You merely have to listen. Pleasure is the law."—also turned to the past to recover what he considered lost musical values.  Debussy asked, "Where are the old harpsichordists who had so much true music? They had the secret of gracefulness and emotion without epilepsy, which we have negated like ungrateful children."  He paid the Baroque masters obvious tribute (in, for example, *Suite Bergamasque*), but there are also subtle manifestations of Debussy's admiration of Baroque qualities throughout his music. The elegance and clarity learned from Couperin and Rameau permanently affected Debussy's aesthetic, even in such exotic excursions as *Pagodes* or *Et la lune descend sur le temple qui fût* ("And the moon descends over the temple that was").

Arnold Schoenberg, too, found time future contained in time past. His invention of twelve-tone serialism is best understood as an extension of German musical traditions in an attempt to assure a new classicism. He moved forward and backward simultaneously, the traditions securing his footing as he reached into the unknown. Schoenberg wrote works "in the olden style" (suites Op. 24, 25 and 29) where well-worn forms set boundaries for his innovations. Perhaps, more important than his frequent use of conventional forms is the fact that Schoenberg never broke free of nineteenth-century tonality's phrasing. Schoenberg "liberated dissonance" and conceived a new approach to the organization of intervals, but remained fiercely faithful to a classical concept of form as thematic development. Later in life, Schoenberg occasionally returned to tonality (composing such works as the 1934 *Suite* for string orchestra and *Kol Nidre*). He wrote in 1948, at the age of seventy-four: "...a longing to return to the older style was always vigorous in me."

Although Igor Stravinsky's historical awareness is usually dubbed "Neoclassicism", it was more far-reaching than that unfortunate catch phrase implies. In his *Symphony of Psalms*, Stravinsky creates a unique synthetic musical universe by richly integrating sonorities, polyphonic textures and modes of the Middle Ages, Renaissance and the twentieth century. "Dumbarton Oaks" pays obvious homage to Bach, specifical-ly the third Brandenburg Concerto, beginning with the parodistic opening phrase of the work. *The Rake's Progress,* an opera inspired by the work of the eighteenth-century English artist William Hogarth, is firmly rooted in Mozartian method. A harpsichord is employed for recitatives, and the opera is structured as a set of arias, reprises of arias and ensembles. The opera's melodic and harmonic language is informed at every level by classical aesthetics. Perhaps, the most intriguing and self-conscious example of an historically aware approach to composition is to be found in Stravinsky's *Agon.* Here, Stravinsky plays a fantastic game, a contest of historical perspectives and methods: medieval counterpoint, Renaissance dance forms, Baroque fanfare, Classical tonality, Romantic chromaticism and contemporary serialism. It is another of Stravinsky's unique synthetic fabrics — a tapestry woven of threads from the entire history of European musical syntax. Neoclassicism doesn't begin to describe it. Stravinsky's historical awareness resulted in a new kind of musical ritualism: detached, precise, vivid, primal.

The distinctive modernity of Olivier Messiaen is richly informed by ancient Greek, medieval European and Hindu rhythmic procedures. His concept of rhythm, including the symbolic aspects of rhythm, resulted in part from a study of the 120 provincial rhythms listed in the thirteenth-century *Salgita-Ratnakara* by Carnagadeva. Messiaen also studied Chopin's free-falling ornamental cascades, Stravinsky's independent rhythmic blocks and Debussy's floating rhythmic clouds. Taking his cue from Stravinsky, who managed to integrate varied approaches to tonality, serialism and modality, Messiaen developed an elaborate personal harmonic language. Drawing on techniques from many cultures and traditions, both ancient and modern, Messiaen constructed a musical method more thorough in nature, but less systematic, than Schoenberg's. His approach defined a rich palette of not only melodic and harmonic principles, but also of rhythmic and timbral processes. The mystical perspective of an impassioned, subjective Catholic worldview is palpable in Messiaen's music. It is spiritual in its depiction of awe, terror, mystery, merciful tenderness and ecstasy. It is theological in its precision of method and rigorous sense of order.

Arvo Pärt and John Tavener, like Messiaen, express their religious orthodoxy through music. Unlike Messiaen, both these composers write music that, while clearly of our time, seems to spring directly from European medieval and Renaissance music, as if the years between then and now never existed. By rooting a contemporary musical language in that of an ancient period when the church's power was nearly absolute, a strange ritualistic power emerges. The music seems at once archaic and daring, impersonal yet passionate.

Even a radical modernist such as Elliott Carter owes much of his thinking to historical concepts and techniques. The composer himself has explained that his rhythmic and contrapuntal innovations, hallmarks of his ultramodern language, can be traced to the rigorously independent style of polyphony of medieval composers such as Ockeghem and Machaut, as well as to Indian and Balinese rhythms ("especially the accelerating Gangsar and Rangkep", he noted), Watusi music, Italian music of the *quattrocento*, and more recent music by Scriabin and Ives.

Toru Takemitsu brought together ancient Japanese instruments and musical concepts with twentieth-century European aesthetics. But his is an art of confrontation rather than integration. His musical works, in which these traditions co-exist, are neither pastiches nor collages, but juxtapositions or simultaneities. Takemitsu, like the Chinese composer Chou Wen-chung who studied with Varèse, not only viewed the past through the present, but confronted two cultures as well. For them, the ancient music of their countries was a living tradition, and contemporary Western music was a frontier. Chou and Takemitsu have created a pioneering, seminal body of work that has had a profound influence on the next generation of Asian composers, such as Tan Dun, Qigang Chen and Bun-Ching Lam.

All this is not to say that using forms and procedures of the past necessarily gives meaning to ideas. Traditional forms cannot provide trivial musical ideas with authenticity, just as a good plan for a house will come to nothing if it is constructed of poor materials. George Bernard Shaw thought that Brahms "dressed himself up" as Beethoven and Bach in this way. Shaw warned the public not to fall for Brahms's playacting: not to imagine that "it's the cowl that makes the monk." Angered by Brahms's return to classicism, Shaw missed the power and passion of the ideas and the progressive nature of the harmonies that were supported by traditional pillars. Shaw was wrong concerning Brahms, but he did colorfully articulate a musical issue that was to dominate twentieth-century composition. There have been many composers who turned to classical forms in desperation, like squatters moving into abandoned houses. Shaw's description of Brahms would be better suited to composers such as Hans Pfitzner, especially in his bloated chamber music, or David Diamond, whose frequent use of sonata-allegro for first movements and grandiose fugal textures in final movements sounds like pompous posturing. Composers who, like politicians, seem to be driven by a concern with their own place in history and who, like many critics, imagine art as a parade of masterpieces created by titans, ironically undermine the real importance of the past: a source of continual renewal.

All the music that a composer has heard becomes memory and forms language, without which musical thinking is impossible. The selection process known as creativity is based on a sense of authenticity, or inner truth. We discover truth in a piece of music and so, as composers, we identify with the gestures of that music, which become integral to our own musical imagination.

Although I had written many canons as exercises while at Juilliard, I had not felt that there was a compelling context for canonic technique in my music for many years. Double canons seemed like fascinating but archaic and artificial musical puzzles. In composing, even the thought of using such a device never occurred to me. Not until I composed my fourth quartet, that is. Unlike most of my music, the fourth quartet was consciously composed *about* a real life event. Normally, I will think in music when composing; extra-musical concepts do not enter the process (even if I discover, after the work is complete, what may have been the catalyst). But in the case of the fourth quartet, I set out from the start to compose a work about the shock, denial, sorrow, hope and resignation connected with a friend's disease. In the final movement, I wanted to compose music of acceptance — not of the disease, but of the terrifying fact that we are not rulers of our destiny. Somehow, the music should say, "There's a divinity that shapes our ends." It should be music that relinquishes control and accepts the idea that control is impossible. A canon would serve the purpose: by its very nature, it conveys the message I sought. Once it is clear that a canon is in progress, the listener accepts the "fate" of the initial music, paralleling the experience of acceptance in the face of illness. To intensify the drama of the music, I composed not a single-voiced theme, but music in two voices. This gave rise to a double canon, since both voices were caught in the web. To achieve the serenity and dignity the subject required, I used medieval modes. The four-part harmonies that result once the double canon is in full swing, however, are far removed from medieval music. Composing this movement was a transforming experience for me. What had previously been historical information (*double canon technique*) was now personal, essential to my thinking about life and musical meaning.

We now live in a multi-dimensional, pluralistic musical world. Unlike previous generations, we have available all of the music the world has produced and continues to produce. There is no dominant school of thought, even concerning basic questions of musical grammar. A composer today may choose to work in any kind of tonal, modal, atonal or rhythmic language, or combine them in any way. This daunting and inviting array of choices is a great challenge to the imagination. It is almost as if we had memories of more than one childhood in several countries at various times in history. The only way to proceed is to start from within: the cadence of our breath, the pulse of our blood, the natural music of the body, the counterpoint of mind.

# Tragedy and Prophesy:

## franz schubert's vision

Franz schubert sought relief from his physical and emotional suffering in drinking binges, sexual experimentation and — luckily for us — his art. In order to translate his pain into adequately expressive and powerful music, Schubert pushed contemporary compositional technique into new territory. In the slow movement of his String Quartet in G Major, D. 887 (Op. Posth. 161), Schubert, in order to convey the depth of his anxiety, wrote a few brief passages in a harmonic idiom previously unknown in music — a technique so radical that it does not surface again until the twentieth century. This important modern compositional technique, later known as octatonicism, was used extensively and redefined by Igor Stravinsky, who was introduced to it by Rimsky-Korsakov. That Schubert employed this technique at all is not a commonly held view among musicologists, but as a composer, I am convinced of it. To explore the musical breakthrough in a meaningful way, we first need to understand the nature of Franz Schubert's suffering.

While it is a cliché that composers of genius suffer for their art, and that great art is born of this suffering, the cliché is not without foundation. All human beings suffer in one way or another. What distinguishes the artist is not *that* he suffers, or even how much he suffers, but that through his art, he has a means of confronting his pain, and that through a creative act, his suffering becomes a life-affirming symbol for others. Creativity is the natural enemy of suffering and death. A work of art promises its creator the possibility of cultural immortality, and what better weapon do we have against our certain death? For a composer who suffers, music offers a spiritual cure. Composition functions as an exorcism.

In 1824, Franz Schubert wrote in his notebook: "Pain sharpens the understanding and strengthens the mind, whereas joy seldom troubles about the former and softens or trivializes the latter." Schubert wrote from personal experience, for he suffered terribly from what is now thought to have been cyclothymia, a kind of manic depression. The playwright Eduard von Bauernfeld, who knew Schubert well during the last years of the composer's life, wrote that Schubert was "vigorous and pleasure-loving", but that "there were also times when a black-winged demon of sorrow and melancholy sought his company—not altogether an evil spirit, it is true, since, in the dark consecrated hours, it often brought out songs of the most agonizing beauty." When he was nineteen, the composer noted in his diary, "Moments of bliss brighten this dark life; over yonder these blissful moments coalesce and are transformed into continuous joy, and happier ones still will turn into visions of yet happier worlds, and so on." At the age of twenty-five, Schubert contracted syphilis, and, from then on, he endured protracted episodes of depression and anxiety, with shorter and shorter periods of relief. Schubert was caught in a cycle of behaviors.

To relieve his depression and loneliness, he would drink. Drinking binges led to anti-social behavior, including sudden rages, during which he would break cups, glasses and plates. His rages led to isolation and loneliness.

During the composition of the String Quartet in G Major, D. 887, the black-winged demon of sorrow and melancholy became Schubert's muse. It is in the *Andante un poco mosso* that the demon appears, heralded by a tragic *fortissimo* c minor chord in the second violin, viola and cello, and a violent upward surging scale in the first violin. Soon after this, Schubert gives us a phrase of music that is so tragic in mood and startling in its manner of utterance that its raw power is shocking even today. As with all music, emotional power is embodied in the technique that expresses it. In this extraordinary passage (and its return in two telling transpositions), Schubert stretched the tonal language of his time to the breaking point, and, in doing so, gives us a glimpse of a harmonic method of our own century. I believe that he knew what he had done, and that he tells us so in the writing.

In order to describe the music in question, I will have to resort to some technical language, a practice counter to my usual style. While the technical description is vital to *proving* my theory, it is not necessary to make the larger point. If the technical jargon becomes incomprehensible to you, brave reader, you will not suffer by ignoring it. Just as it is possible to understand that a smile caused by true emotion is different than a forced smile-for-the-camera without knowing how one's limbic cortices and basal ganglia work, my thesis can be understood without the following technical evidence.

Schubert's impassioned, ground-breaking music begins (in measure 52) with two notes (G and B-Flat) in the first violin and viola, which appear, violently, like the black-winged demon itself in the unsuspecting air. This pair of notes (the demon's call?) appears three times in this passage, clearly delineating the phrase structure. What is immediately shocking about this pair of notes is that *they do not change as the harmonies do.* These notes hang in the air as a signal that something extraordinary is occurring in the music. The notes refuse to give way harmonically in the expected manner, creating an emotional dissonance unprecedented in the art. Remarkably, these notes are simultaneously unprecedented in conception and immediately comprehensible; they are shocking yet obviously right. The ability to create such music is the mark of genius. But this is only the beginning.

The trembling harmonies that are framed by the demonic dyad descend in a series of minor thirds (E – C Sharp – B Flat – G), eerily presenting half cadences as it goes. We are, then, presented with a diminished seventh chord as an outline for the harmonic progression. The half-cadences, necessarily, land on three major chords also linked by minor third transpositions. *If this passage were presented only once*, it would not in itself suggest an awareness of symmetrical harmonic thinking built on diminished seventh chords, which is the essence of octatonicism. The passage appears again (measures 72–79), transposed down a half-step, to the next level of diminished seventh harmony. This begins to suggest a conscious awareness of the possibilities of this technique, but it might also be the result of typically classical symmetry and formal balance (in the structural sense). But then the passage appears a *third time* (measures 131–139), transposed down to the remaining diminished seventh chord, but *not the obvious* choice. Rather, it is transposed up a perfect fifth from the original. This completes the harmonic cycle but simultaneously allows for the necessary modulation to the dominant of the key. *The fact that this passage appears in all three possible transpositions reveals that Schubert was fully conscious of the technique as a symmetrical division of the total chromatic spectrum.* He was not merely using diminished seventh chords as so many composers before him have. Schubert was on to the unexplored emotional power inherent in the symmetrical partitioning of all twelve tones. This technique generates new and startling harmonic connections; just what the doctor ordered.

The two demonic notes, of course, appear in each section transposed along with the rest of the music. But, as in the initial passage, the two demonic notes are not transposed *within* the newly transposed version, but remain stuck, terrifying in their defiance of tonal normalcy. This concept is like a red flag to the analyst. Schubert's black-winged demon brought with him some special magic, something new to the craft, meant only for the future. And Schubert — desperate, tortured Schubert — seized the technique gratefully, recognizing in its strangeness the agonizing beauty he sought to express. Pain had sharpened his understanding and strengthened his mind.

# A Composer's Music Therapy

Early on, during my two years of psychotherapy, I offered my psychiatrist tickets to one of my concerts. He refused, and asked me, "Is it important to you that I hear your music?" I said that I thought it was. He countered, "Don't you think you are a worthwhile person aside from your work?" I was a bit flustered by this response. He insisted that he did not want to know anything about me other than what I revealed to him during our sessions. I left his office and strolled home through Central Park, wondering if my offer of tickets was a power play of some sort on my part. Did I need to have him in my audience? Was it impossible for me to relate to him without his first being *impressed* by my music? Couldn't he understand me as a person without my work?

While I was convinced at the time that he was right, that his knowing my music would interfere with the purity of our sessions, I now wonder whether that was too conventional a reaction, the standard line of psychiatrists. What if I were not in therapy to explore my inner life, but because I was suffering from clinical depression or schizophrenia? Would my doctor *still* not want to know what my work was like? Imagine a depressed, lonely, angry person who manages to create brilliant, inspiring, joyous works of art. If Beethoven had had a psychiatrist, would the doctor have listened to his patient's music? Beethoven the man, *minus* the music, tells a very different story indeed.

Music reveals much about a composer's inner life, and often profoundly expresses what the composer cannot or will not say in words. What a composer *cannot* say in words will likely surface in the music *unconsciously*. What a composer *will not* say in words is more likely to surface more intentionally in the music. This depends, of course, on the extent to which a composer is consciously aware of meaning in his music at all. Sometimes clues from the composer's life reveal new meanings in the music to listeners. At times, we can hear the music as a unique and vivid document of events in the composer's life, whether or not the composer *consciously* meant it to be so.

We know that Beethoven consciously knew that he was composing music about his deafness when he wrote the Opus 59 string quartets, dedicated to Count Razamouvsky, because he wrote on the manuscript of Opus 59, No. 1 "Let my deafness no longer be a secret—even in my art." We might say upon hearing a poorly composed piece, that the composer seemed to be deaf, but how can a piece of music be great and also be about deafness? If the music sounds tortured, anguished and tragic, we might decide that the composer wrote it because his deafness made him feel that way. But a composer who is miserable for any reason other than deafness might also have written such music. Where exactly in the music can we perceive the deafness rather than a more common anguish?

An answer may be found in the scherzo to Opus 59, No. 1. Here Beethoven is able to find a kind of black humor in his own deafness. The opening "theme" has only one note. It is literally monotonic, like a deaf person's unmodulated, uninflected speech. This pathetic utterance, which caused laughter and mockery in Beethoven's time, is answered by a graceful, though somewhat prosaic, melodic phrase. The alternation of the monotonic comment and the response is quickly established as a conversation among the instruments, in the great tradition of quartet writing. Here, however, it is not merely conversational in style, but a dramatic reenactment of real conversation. One can easily imagine Beethoven and his cronies huddled about a table, drinking and eating and arguing. Beethoven's friends occasionally have to shout to make themselves understood by the deaf composer, and they whisper among themselves, making rude asides and jokes. Beethoven's uninflected speech probably caused both concern and cruel laughter, and he would burst out yelling when he felt that he was being taken advantage of or mocked by his drunken friends. Beethoven had a conversation notebook with him for whenever the discussion might require written clarification, but for the best record of the nature of his conversations, we should turn to the music itself.

It may be argued that this is typical scherzo writing, that it is in the tradition of the scherzo, which after all means *prank* in Italian, for composers to write sudden dynamic outbursts, comic melodies and quick changes of mood. But Beethoven's scherzos are distinguished by their remarkable *realism* rather than by any mere convention. Beethoven's greatness lies in his ability to bring to *life* (a meaningful expression here) concepts and forms that would be merely conventional in a lesser composer's hands. I like to think that he not only brings forms to life, but that he *brings his real life to* forms. The mood changes of this scherzo are extraordinary because they tell of his real emotional instability. The drama and black comedy of his deafness at a table in a public drinking house can be heard throughout the movement. Even the purposeful wrong notes, just before the final chords, are not mere wisecracks, but painful taunts, mocking the struggle of a deaf composer as he searches for the right notes.

If we can envision Beethoven's psychiatrist learning about his patient by listening to the music, we can also imagine how a perceptive therapist (with a musical background) might analyze Prokofiev from knowing both his life and work. Prokofiev's classic for children, *Peter and the Wolf,* may be seen as the quickest path to understanding the composer's personality. The story of the naughty boy, who ignores his grandfather's warning yet eventually triumphs, tells us almost as much as the music does about the composer's disregard for authority and convention, his ambition to stand out from the crowd, and his nose-thumbing "dare you to stop me" self-confidence. When he was a young conservatory student, Prokofiev had the obnoxious habit of keeping records of other students' assignments, mistakes, corrections from teachers and grades. Younger than most of the other students in his class, the precocious boy-wonder also argued with his teachers. No teacher was brilliant enough or creative enough to be worth his time. But the students disliked his constant interference with their work. He was even attacked by an angry student in the hallway, and he had to be rescued by a larger boy, who didn't like to see even the annoying little know-it-all bullied.

Prokofiev's fascination with mistakes in harmony and counterpoint assignments goes beyond being a good student. It is the fixation of a mind obsessed with the allure of error, of being caught doing something wrong. I imagine it as a kind of vertigo—a fear of his own desire to fall into the abyss of forbidden harmony. He was so afraid of being a bad student (as if that meant bad *boy*), that he took on the role of musical police in the classroom while being as upright and as correct as humanly possible. As the composer developed his own harmonic style, it seemed to be about musical misbehaving: naughty and sarcastic dissonances, mischievous modulations and forbidden resolutions. His imagination was wonderfully linked to his memory, as it must be with every artist. But his memories were those of a precocious schoolboy, eager to please the teacher (audiences), while taunting other students (competing composers) and thumbing his nose at everyone who didn't understand him (critics).

In his music, Prokofiev was himself the true Peter, writ large, of the children's folk tale. Stalin was, to say the least, the ultimate authority figure; he was both the forbidding grandfather and the terrorizing wolf. Prokofiev, when he returned to Stalin's Soviet Union from the United States, was not able to catch the wolf, but rather was caught himself. This composer of daring bravura, of penetrating power and bittersweet dissonances, of unrelenting energy and snide grotesquerie, was crushed by one of our century's cruelest madmen. In the end, Peter (Prokofiev) and the wolf (Stalin) died on the same day, a great irony of which they were both unaware.

Even more than Prokofiev, Shostakovich lived in the shadow of Stalin. A tortured artist, Shostakovich kept the truth for his music, for it was too risky to speak it. A psychiatrist, hoping to learn anything significant about Shostakovich, would have to have heard his music or at the very least, witnessed the composer in performance. Michael Ignatieff, in his book on the philosopher Isaiah Berlin, tells a revealing story of Shostakovich during his 1958 visit to Oxford, where he was to receive an honorary degree. In England, Shostakovich was usually accompanied by Soviet handlers. When these men were around, Shostakovich called them his "dear friends". Those who saw him there described him as nervous, withdrawn, repressed, shy. At a musical evening at Oxford, the composer was described by the philosopher, Isaiah Berlin, as "huddling in the corner like a frightened animal." But when Berlin suggested that Shostakovich play the piano, the composer was utterly transformed, revealing a passionate and fiery persona. Shostakovich released his rage through his music. There, in a language clear and uncompromising, yet elusive and confusing to the non-initiated, he could curse tyrants and cry out for justice. While his music shares some of the taunting, mocking and grotesque characteristics of Prokofiev's work, Shostakovich's music is more pained, hardened. There is in much of it an unspeakable bleakness. Unspeakable in words, but vivid in music.

In psychotherapy, one hopes for catharsis. A vivid recollection, and the connecting of emotional dots will, hopefully, lead to a sense of liberation or transcendence. There may be a feeling of cleansing the soul after the patient finally admits a long-hidden transgression, releases pent-up rage, comes to a surprising realization or articulates a formerly elusive emotion. The feeling is, finally, that we have learned something — one of the finest feelings there is. In music, there is always the imminent possibility of transcendence and liberation, even in the expression of pain, misery or despair. This is because it is, by its very nature, joyous to create and to perform, and from every clear artistic expression, we learn about ourselves.

Years ago, I attended a master class in French art song at Juilliard. A young baritone placed one hand on the piano and began to sing Fauré's "Au cimetière" ("At the Cemetery"), a morbid and melancholy song. Soon, he was stopped by the teacher, an elderly, petite French woman with an air of elegance and grace about her. "You are too sad, too disturbed, too miserable. Where is the joy?" she asked the young man. Utterly perplexed, the young man responded, "But this is a song about death. Why should there be joy in it?" With a sigh through pursed lips and slightly raised shoulders, the teacher answered, "There is joy because it is a song, because the poetry is eloquent, and the music is beautiful. There is joy because it is art. Again, please." This was a very lucky baritone who had just learned the difference between performance and real life in a single stroke.

What might my psychiatrist have learned from hearing

my music that he never discovered? In the end, it does not matter what he would have learned, only what I, the patient, would have gained. Is there something lurking in the music that I never articulated in my sessions, that I, perhaps, was unaware of consciously, verbally? Recently, Robert Hesson, a critic I have never met, wrote a review of my music for Stereophile magazine in which he articulated something about my music that shocked me because it rang true and seemed fundamental to my work, yet I had never thought of it myself. He wrote, "There is a paradoxical feeling that you are always in familiar territory, although surrounded by an enveloping strangeness." Suddenly, I was made aware of a crucial aspect of my musical thinking that informed almost all of my decisions at a subconscious level: "familiar territory surrounded by an enveloping strangeness" perfectly described the delicate balance of my never-before-articulated aesthetic. How I loved to create subtle detours in well-traveled musical roads! I was wary of both the avant-garde and the conservative, unattracted by experimentalism, yet bored by the commonplace. By the same token, I was intrigued by both neo-classical and radical ideas. But never had I consciously used a "familiar" concept or technique and deliberately twisted or contorted it. Now, because of this review, I was, for a brief period, made self-conscious of this way of hearing my music, which made me uneasily aware of my thought process while composing. Only by working myself into a state of purely musical thought, could I leave behind these vivid, perceptive words.

But more to the point is the question: Did this fundamental musical insight add to my perception of myself as a human being, not "just" as a composer (as my therapist would have said)? It did. I have long been in the habit of thinking about how my music relates to my life, and so Hesson's observation naturally led me to examine the connection in a new light. "Familiar territory surrounded by an enveloping strangeness" certainly has resonance with the fact that I have been married three times, to name one powerful example. Just as with my music, I want both the traditional arrangement and the singular experience, the middle-class life and the radical, artist's existence. In my professional life, too, I deal in the familiar and strange as a highly visible representative of the musical establishment (as a lecturer and education director at the Chamber Music Society of Lincoln Center), and as a member of that strange, forever-on-the-fringe group of American musicians, misunderstood and ignored by many (and listened to by few), known as composers. This is often made plain to me when, after I have given a lecture on Mozart or Beethoven, a member of the audience confides in me how she wishes that composers today could write listenable music, expecting me — a man clearly devoted to the classics — to agree. How familiar, how strange.

I learned a great deal from psychotherapy, and yet this deceptively simple comment by a music critic — which unexpectedly united my music and my life choices — affirmed my original assumption that in music we can discover the rest of the story: the unspoken, mysterious aspects of the self that are at least as real as what we can say. The music matters.

# Song, Dance and Cherry Blossoms
## in the Wind

A MONG MUSICIANS, it is commonly agreed that highly structured musical forms may be traced back to one of two basic impulses: to dance or to sing. For much music, especially Western music until the time of Debussy, this is true. Even in Beethoven's late string quartets — considered by musicians to be the height of classical composition in richness of ideas, emotional intensity and inspired architecture — we can affirm the importance of basic song and dance roots: the most intriguing, and obvious, example being Opus 130, with its series of Baroque-like dances and the impassioned aria of the *Cavatina*. The sonata form as molded by Papa Haydn is a narrative structure descended from Baroque dance forms. The simple binary and ternary forms of the court dances (*Allemande, Corrente, Sarabande, Gigue, etc.*) grew larger, and incorporated the elements of drama: contrast, transition and development. One might think of the change as a movement from folk dances to ballet, even to large-scale story ballets. The original impulse to dance is refined and given a story form. Slow movements are the descendents of lullabies and love songs.

The song and dance impulses of Western music, from the Renaissance until the late nineteenth century, are responsible for giving us the regular meters of common time (so-called for a reason) and triple time. The regular, predictable pulse of this music has been an accepted fact of musical discourse for hundreds of years in the West. The clip-clop of horses' hooves and the tramp-tramp of the royal troops on parade or going off to battle were ingrained in the general musical consciousness, along with the rocking lullabies crooned by mothers and grandmothers everywhere. The beat underneath all of this is the thump of the human heart, the pulse of our blood. But the tick of our clocks and the gongs of great bells in the centers of towns and villages also tell us that time marches, not floats, on.

Silence, in this worldview, is the space between ticks and tocks. It is the moment between heartbeats heard in a stethescope, it is the waiting for the other shoe to drop. Silence is merely what is unarticulated. The momentary lift of the bow from the violin between phrases, the hand raised from the keyboard in order to precisely time the next musical sound: these are the silences of song and dance impulses. There are, of course, some dramatic pauses in narrative music that draw their power from the very fact of their rarity. Silence, in Haydn and Mozart, for example, will serve to punctuate structural points of interest, like specially shaped bricks that surround windows or delineate the floors on the facade of a building. There are silences *between* movements of a sonata, but those silences are not generally considered part of the piece. With rare exceptions, such as where the final chord of a movement is meant to usher in the beginning of the next movement, the pauses between movements are opportunities for audiences to cough, musicians to tune and late-comers to find their seats.

Stops and silences in the forward ticking of baroque and classical works are so rare that when they do appear, they are very powerful. Such silences are often used for comic effect, as in many a Haydn scherzo, or to strike fear into the suddenly-stopped heart of the listener, as in Beethoven's *Coriolanus Overutre*, or as a moment for a *cadenza*. *Cadenzas* are important not only because they give the performer a moment of bravura, but because they offer a suspension of time, a moment of freedom from pulse. Here the composer will place a *fermata* over a chord, a "hold", as it is commonly called, which signifies a suspension of rhythmic movement. Then, the composer will write the *cadenza* in small notes, a telling tradition. The small notes symbolize rhythmic and therefore *emotional* freedom. They are beloved of musicians, these tiny notes, for their immediate licence to ignore the speed limit. Like the snooze button on an alarm clock, the tiny notes offer a relief from measured time — a moment of sensuous, dreamy otherworldliness, before the tick-tock of consciousness resumes.

But this is not the only way to view the world, nor is it the only way that music is written. Consider the following poem:

How can I blame the cherry blossoms
for rejecting this floating world
and driftng away as the wind calls them?

The poem is by a Japanese woman of the thirteenth-century, who signed her poems "Shunzei's Daughter", translated by Kenneth Rexroth and Ikuko Atsumi. The two images in the poem—that of the floating world (as Japan is typically called) and the cherry blossoms drifting away in the wind—are both free from pulse. The poem has only one action, the drifting cherry blossoms, but it also communicates a complex state of mind as the observer subtly relates this fleeting moment to a desired freedom from "this floating world." A melancholy existence and a desire for liberation are expressed powerfully by the extraordinary idea that the cherry blossoms are rejecting the world to follow the wind. Like a gentle cadenza between chords in a slow movement of Haydn or Mozart, this gesture of a poem offers a moment of deep reflection. Music that could capture the images in this poem would itself have to be floating, drifting, free of the weight of pulse. In this music, silence would necessarily attain a greater significance in the absence of pulse and regular meter.

While a richly developed harmonic language, a multifac-eted contrapuntal method and metaphorically charged formal designs had evolved in Europe, there was in the East a music of subtle rhythmic intricacy and a refined sense of sonority for its own sake. Debussy wrote in 1895: "Do you not remember the Javanese music able to express every nuance of meaning, even unmentionable shades, and which make our tonic and dominant seem like empty phantoms for the use of unwise infants?" Javanese, Chinese and Japanese music great-ly influenced the development of French music in the early 1900's. Some of this was a genuine fascination with exotic musical concepts and techniques, while there was also a kind of intoxication with an imaginary idea of the Orient, as the opening lines of Tristan Klingsor's text for Ravel's Scheherazade clearly demonstrate:

"Asia, Asia, Asia,
ancient land of wonder, of nursery tales
where fantasy may sleep like an empress
in her forest full of mystery."

In the latter part of the twentieth century, the circle has been completed: the French music that was so richly informed by the music of the East now influenced a new generation of Asian composers.

The Japanese composer Toru Takemitsu, who is known to audiences worldwide for his innovative and emotionally charged film scores for the director Akira Kurosawa, and who remains the most renowned of Japanese composers, was profoundly influenced by the harmonic and ochestral techniques of Debussy and Messiaen. But what Takemitsu has brought into his very personal musical language is the rhythm of the cherry blossoms drifting in the wind, away from the floating world. His use of silence is palpably Eastern. In *Confronting Silence*, a book of selected writings by Takemitsu, the composer describes the concept of *ma*, a "point of intense silence" that precedes a single stroke of the strings or even one plucked tone. Takemitsu writes, "It is here that sound and silence confront each other, balancing each other in a relationship beyond any objective measurement." A fine example of the power of silence in Takemitsu's music can be heard in *Quatrain II*, written for the ensemble Tashi (Peter Serkin, piano; Ida Kavafian, violin; Richard Stoltzman, clarinet; Fred Sherry, cello). *Quatrain II* is a transcription for quartet alone of the original version, *Quatrain*, which featured the members of Tashi as soloists with orchestra. Takemitsu considered Messiaen as his spiritual mentor, and was profoundly affected by the French composer's masterpiece *Quartet for the End of Time*, which he heard Tashi perform and discuss with Messiaen. In *Quatrain*, written for the same instruments as the *Quartet for the End of Time* plus orchestra (and in *Quatrain II*), Takemitsu included an eight-measure homage to Messiaen. It is music that captures the delicate timbral beauty of Messiaen's music in finely etched, sonorous piano chords and dreamy glissandos in the violin and cello, with a slowly arching ethereal melody in the clarinet. The climactic moment in the music is a grand pause, a giant *ma*. This breathtaking silence is often heard as a reference to the grand silences in the music of Messiaen, as if it were another form of tribute by Takemitsu. But we must remember that Messiaen's personal aesthetic was profoundly influenced by Eastern music. Again, the circle is completed.

Silence in the music of Messiaen and Takemitsu is awe-inspiring, but it is not the dramatic, suspenseful silence of Beethoven's *Coriolanus* overture. Takemitsu's silence is about the sound of silence itself (Simon and Garfunkel notwithstanding). It is about the essence of silence, the drama of silence in human experience. Takemitsu wrote: "The fear of silence is nothing new. Silence surrounds the dark world of death. Sometimes the silence of the vast universe hovers over us, enveloping us." Takemitsu considers art to be a rebellion against silence, a resistance to silence.

Takemitsu was an admirer of John Cage, who famously

made use of silence with his piece 4'33" (1952). This work, performable by any musician with any instrument, consists of the player sitting silently for four minutes and thirty-three seconds, while the audience, supposedly, listens to the sounds around them with new awareness. In a fitting choreographic interpretation of the piece, Paul Taylor and his dance partner, Betty De Jong, both dressed in formal evening clothes, and stood motionless on stage for four minutes and thirty-three seconds. The next day, *the New York Times* printed its review: a completely blank column. Cage's use of silence, though meant seriously, was given a comic patina by the work's title; for the concept of exact timing framed the silence as a theatrical event, even suggesting a sports event, and removed the possibility of its natural power. While Cage achieved one goal —Western concert audiences confronting silence head on— the piece remains a prank.

In Takemitsu's music, such as *Quatrain II*, silence is approached with reverence, and the listener is taken on a journey toward the moment of stillness, like wind dying away in a bamboo grove. The quiet reverberates with the just-heard music of the ensemble, but it also resonates with our own sudden awareness of the void. It attains gracefully what Cage's piece jabs at awkwardly: the transcendent music of stillness.

In a work of Bach, Haydn, Mozart or Beethoven, a silence will necessarily be an interruption of tempo. But in Eastern music, such as Takemitsu's, there has been no pulse, no ongoing foot-tapping tempo, so we do not feel the silence as a suspension of time. A kind of perceptual inversion happens: *we feel the music as ripples in the surface of silence.*

This inversion has great emotional power, pulling us into a hushed confrontation with our own beating hearts, the unheard pulse that roars beneath our skin.

Consider these lines, again translated by Kenneth Rexroth and Ikuko Atsumi, by the eleventh-century Japanese woman poet Ise Tayu:

Only the waning morning moon

visits my garden

where no lover comes.

For Ise Tayu, the garden is not merely empty, for it is there that the moon wanes and no lover comes. Nothingness trembles with meaning. Nature's silence resounds with human desire.

We can hear it in Takemitsu's music: the unsung song, the dance that will never be danced, the sound of blameless cherry blossoms drifting away as the wind calls them.

# WHALES IN CONCERT HALLS:
## SOME THOUGHTS ON GEORGE CRUMB

G EORGE CRUMB'S *Vox Balanae* (*Voice of the Whale*) begins with a "Vocalise for the beginning of time" that is played on the flute and sung, simultaneously, by the flutist — a typically eerie and provocative sound in the extraordinary Crumb arsenal of sonic innovation. The Vocalise ends with a reference to Richard Strauss's *Also Sprach Zarathustra* . The ensuing variations on the Sea Theme are provocatively entitled: *Archeozoic (var. 1); Proterozoic (var. 2.); Paleozoic (var. 3); Mesozoic (var. 4); Cenozoic (var. 5).* Variation 5, the Cenozoic period, in which humans appear on the planet, is marked "Dramatic; with a sense of imminent destiny" by the composer. At this point, the *Zarathustra* reference reappears.

George Crumb's music reveals what is primal, elemental, essential. While all music moves in time, this work is aesthetically and thematically about time itself. Like Messiaen's *Quartet for the End of Time*, this trio for the "beginning of time" inspires awe with powerful eruptions of rhythm and the suspension of musical pulse. But unlike Messiaen's Catholic-inspired work, Crumb's *Voice of the Whale* is a-theological. It is physical — its spirituality is derived from the sense of wonder that Albert Einstein spoke of when he said:

"The most beautiful and profound emotion we can experience is the sensation of the mystical. It is the sower of all true science. To know that what is impenetrable to us really exists, manifesting itself as the highest wisdom and the most radiant beauty, which our dull faculties can comprehend only in their primitive forms—this knowledge, this feeling, is at the center of true religion."

Ludwig Wittgenstein put it this way: "The mystical is not how the world is, but *that* it is." T.S. Eliot described the role of the poet in a way that relates to the music of George Crumb. Eliot wrote:

"The poet possesses the feeling for syllable and rhythm, penetrating far below the conscious levels of thought and feeling, invigorating every word; sinking to the most primitive and forgotten, returning to the origin and bringing something back, seeking the beginning and the end. It works through meanings, certainly, or not without meanings in the ordinary sense, and fuses the old and obliterated and trite, the current and the new and surprising, the most ancient and the most civilized mentality."

George Crumb's music—along with the masks and lighting he requests—reminds us that music was not originally conceived for the concert hall. Music is central to the spirituality of virtually all folk histories in the world: the Australian Aborigines, the many African and Oceanic tribes, the ancient religious organizations of China, the Vedic rites of India, the Pythagorean philosophers of ancient Greece and the native American tribes. They all thought of music, of *sound* itself, as one of the primeval forces of creation. The writer Jamake Highwater, a descendant of the Blackfeet and

Cherokee tribes, reminds us in his book *The Primal Mind* that this view of music as an aspect of creation is sometimes metaphorical, but it can also be quite literal, as in the folk history of the Tamil people, which relates that the world itself was derived from the tambourine of god. In Jewish cantorial chant, text and occasion are inextricably linked to mode and melody. This kind of music is not about the text, it is not a *setting of the text*, but rather the music is a mystical manifestation of the text's true meaning. George Crumb returns to holistic music. It is music before the very concept of *art*.

A shockingly *original* composer, George Crumb's music paradoxically returns to a musical universe that pre-dates the concept of originality. How can primal music, tribal music, music of the earth and sea be bound by the terms of originality and self-expression? With primal innocence, in a Zen state of mind, Crumb approaches all the instruments freshly, like a child genius. If you have never heard a piano played, what would stop you from plucking strings or dampening their vibrations with your hands, or playing harmonics inside the piano? Glass rods placed inside the piano are used for a stunning effect that, again, suggests the pure, unconventional mind. For Crumb, the instrument itself incites a spiritual journey of sonic, poetic exploration.

This strange and beautiful music has to *happen* somewhere, and that somewhere is the misunderstood edifice known as the concert hall. The concert hall, at best, can be a kind of modern temple, a place of ritual: a cathedral, tipi, longhouse, kiva. Music — for many musicians an all-consuming passion and daily spiritual and physical exercise — is made public in an elaborate ceremony within the concert hall. The ceremony involves such things as formal attire and a very odd, primitive ritual of communal affirmation, consisting of rapidly and repeatedly beating one's palms together. This is performed collectively, but usually without rhythmic coordination. Participants—who are all facing the same direction, but seated— are privately consummating their own internal rhythms within the public hubbub.

The special lighting and masks that are required by Crumb for *Voice of the Whale* suggest a time before the existence of cathedrals and temples, let alone concert halls. The music and ritualistic manner of its presentation conjure up an image of the *sipapu* — or "Earth Navel"—within the Pueblo *kiva*, which is understood to be the center of the world. Crumb reminds us that the concert hall is a *sacred space*, something that is too easily forgotten as we hang our coats over the backs of seats, stuff briefcases and pocketbooks under them, open our programs and flip through pages of advertisements, looking for the evening's program. *Vox Balanae* suggests the natural world in, of course, a theatrical way— and this is another irony. Concert halls and apartment buildings are the work of humans; and humans are part of nature. Our architecture may be more elaborate than an eagle's nest or a beaver's dam, but it is, *like those simple creations*, a natural extension of our nature and our needs.

Before there was the concert hall, there was the music of the church and temple. No tickets were necessary. Music was part of the language of a belief system; it was a liturgy not a literature. Even so, as George Bernard Shaw commented, the clergy has to work pretty hard to get people to attend a church "performance", although it is always free at a "theater" whose doors are always open to all.

Before theology and ritual, there was the music of daily living, of the innately spiritual; one might say of the truly spiritual, that realm before the confusion of tongues and the invention of moral law. For as the Chinese poet Lao Tzu said in the *Tao Te Ching*: "Ritual is the husk of religion." Before theology, there was spiritual music of hunting, war, marriage, death and birth—the music of everyday reality. That is where it all begins, for reality is the only path to mystery.

Going back even further, before humans walked the earth and beat logs (creating the early logarithms), there was the music of other creatures: singing birds, winging through the air; growling, roaring beasts prowling the earth; and, in the ocean, singing whales.

Before the music of creatures, there was the music of the world itself: the slap and roll of oceans, the noisy cracking of splitting rock, the splintering of trees as they were hit by lightning, the rhythms of rain, the counterpoint of seasons throughout the planet, the unimaginably slow crescendo of mountains being born (imagine a metronome mark where a whole note equals an ice age).

George Crumb's music resonates across time, cutting through however many dimensions of space-time there may be, riding the spiral of superstrings, spinning on space-time's coils like a child in a playground, joyously terrified, fully aware without the effort of thought.

The early artists of the cave, the painters of Lasceaux—

or of Pechmerle—revealed to their own community the awesome discoveries of that very afternoon: a bison, a horse, a tiger (something to eat, something to fear). Their art was that of the explorer, the hunter, the warrior, the story-teller, town crier, the newscaster and priest. Their art was the art of discovery and important information: like maps of unexplored lands, fractal images of imaginary landscapes or photographs of the moon.

When Crumb learned in 1969 that whales sang, that they could sing elaborate songs across the ocean, that their concert hall was the watery planet itself, at that moment, the musical explorer in Crumb was inspired to map their melodies. He would tell the world about these artists of the ocean in his own epic poem. Crumb used, as he always does, his own set of sorcerer's symbols in combination with traditional music notation, in order to communicate fresh and strange ideas of his soundscape.

In the end, what do we really know of the whale's songs? Why do they sing? Is their melody all practical—the sounds of courtship, warnings and recommendations of hunting grounds, as some scientists have suggested? Or are these songs *about* courtship, tales of tragedy and celebrations of good hunting? In other words, is this whale music merely information, or is it art? Is it only an outcry of actual lust, fear and hunger, or is it some strangely formalized presentation, the musical resonance of *all* whale lust and love, fear, desire and craving? Is it some ancient ritual or a genetically encoded pitch sequence? Is it the spiritual chant, the ocean psalm of these giant, ancient creatures or just an eerie moan that *suggests* to us our own aloneness, that *reminds* us of our own human music?

We always come back to ourselves, for we are all we can really know— and that's if we're lucky. By taking us on a journey to the beginning of time and into the depths of the ocean, Crumb has brought us back to that unseeable no-place: the human soul.

# MUSICAL ART GALLERY OF THE MIND

IF WE CONSIDER Mozart's mind to be a kind of musical art gallery, then it would be an eighteenth-century European one. There would be no medieval musical art on the walls, nothing from the Renaissance—Baroque works would be stored downstairs in the archives. When Mozart discovered the music of Bach, it was a revelation and an inspiration, yet these works were like dusty unframed canvases stacked against the wall. He had little to curate and much to create.

But as we approach the twenty-first century, we composers must metaphorically stroll through vast mind-museums, comprising an infinity of small galleries. In addition to the more familiar Baroque, Classical, Romantic and Modern exhibits, there are many alluring shows: the Byzantine Chant Pavilion, the Chinese Opera Theater, the African Rhythm Wing, the Secret Chromatic Art of the Netherlands Renaissance Show, the Italian Renaissance Mannerist Display, the Musical Traditions of Japanese Noh Gardens, the Klezmer Room, the New Orleans Blues and Ragtime Hall, the New Jazz Exhibit and other areas of the mind-museum, including the New Age Parlor,  the Minimalist Waiting Area, the Unrepentant Dodecaphonic Cafeteria, the Electronic Storage Room, the Computer Music Space, the Popular Culture

Revolving Doors (where you first come in) and, of course, the permanent Pentatonic Plaza outside, donated by the Sino-Appalachian Committee for the People's Mode.

What all this means is that the word eclectic now describes our musical climate about as meaningfully as the word *dangerous* describes the nuclear bomb. Would Mozart have written anywhere near as much music as he did if his mind-museum was as well-stocked as ours? The questions a composer confronts today are fundamental to musical thinking: *Should my music be tonal or tonally based, modal, modally derived but with a chromatic surface, atonal (chromatic dissonance), serial, twelve-tone, rooted in popular music, derived from the folk music of my ancestors, jazz-related, electronic, structured in received forms, free-associative, Eastern-influenced, neo-something, minimal, maximal, tragical, comical, pastoral, and so on.*

One composer, George Rochberg, developed a language of "differences", as he calls it. This is a music of deliberate stylistic diversity. Rochberg, who, after making a name for himself as a follower of Schoenberg, rejected that heritage and helped to bring back tonality. Many composers who followed Rochberg into diatonic territory might have been afraid to write a major triad without a musical soldier leading the way, or perhaps without a musical therapist telling them it was okay. Rochberg's most recent work, *Eden: Out of Time, Out of Space,* for guitar and sextet (violin, viola, cello, flute, clarinet, horn), is practically an illustration of the Gallery of the Mind concept. The listener is ushered into a strange sound-world of guitar tremolos and long silences. Soon the listener

is guided through a gallery of musical paintings— a dissonant abstract here, a jaunty ragtime scene there, a portrait of
Mahler, a scene from the life of Monteverdi and more. In a
real art gallery, the viewer decides how long to look at any
given work of art. In a piece of music, the composer decides
how long we will listen. In this musical mind-gallery,
Rochberg structures the piece in a kind of anti-form manner,
giving the impression that the piece has no beginning or end,
that it is "out of time" and "out of space", like the imaginary
utopia of Eden.

For me, composing usually involves a period of wandering through the mind-gallery of music, listening to the many
worlds that have become part of my memory, and, thus, part
of my imagination. The Germans have a saying "Who has
choice, has torment." But an artist today, naturally, comes to
terms with this infinity of choices and learns to see it as a gift,
a modern musician's lucky inheritance. We begin to see the
entire history of the music of the world — all its techniques
and metphors, its vocabularies and grammars — as ours for
the taking. This musical gallery of the mind is, after all, made
of thoughts and memories; it has no walls, no floors and no
ceiling. It is truly a musical Eden, and we are, as human mak-
ers of music, lost forever in its beauty.

# LIGHT, LAYERS AND EDGES:

## MUSIC AND THE VISUAL ARTS

ASPECTS OF PAINTING OFTEN SUGGEST musical ideas, especially the interplay of shades of color, the layering of textures and the activity at the very edges of a canvas.

The visual effect of *chiaroscuro* (light and shadow) has
intrigued me musically for some time. It is a perfectly musical concept, and the word would be well adopted into musical terminology to describe the effect of shifting timbres (such
as from strings to winds) and changes in density within a
sonority (doubling of pitches, for example). The use of timbre (the color of sound) in composition has two distinct histories: one primarily Western, the other essentially Eastern. In
the West, composers have tended to consider timbre as an
indicator or illuminator of structure, especially in German
music. The brass will enter in order to present a new theme.
The orchestra will be divided into colors reflecting specific
musical functions: a harmonic texture in the bowed strings,
support below in the plucked basses, a lyrical oboe solo hovering above, and muted brass in occasional punctuation.
Clarity in the presentation of ideas and the delineation of
form is a great benefit of this tradition. The Eastern approach
to musical color, which became an aspect of French music
with Debussy (it is dangerous to paint with too broad a

brush!), is not structural, but independent. The colors of sound exist for the moment, not to illuminate aspects of architecture. In Japanese music, for instance, the sound itself is more significant than its use in expression. A sound is considered complete in itself, as an image of the world, and not as a building block for a linear structure. Even though Arnold Schoenberg's innovative concept of *Klangfarbenmelodie* ("sound-color-melody") focuses the attention on timbre rather than pitch, it is nonetheless a *progression* of tone colors, requiring, as the composer put it, "inner logic" for their construction. The two fundamental approaches to musical color were first integrated in the music of Debussy. Since then, composers have been concerned with both the functional and independent aspects of timbre as part of an international heritage.

Another aspect of painting that has been provocative for me as a composer is "layering", a technique that my brother, Jonathan, has been exploring in his paintings for years. I have tried to compose works that feel like wandering through a dark, multi-layered painting: *Chiaroscuro* (for winds), *By a grace of sense surrounded* (String Quartet No. 1), and *In Memories Of* (for piano and string quartet), among others. Layers of sound are piled up in one area of the music, separated in another, exposed through a crack here, covered thickly there. After all, aren't we ourselves very much that way: layers of memory and experience, some clear, some thickly covered over, some like a ray of brilliant light, others cloudy, vague, possibly frightening?

For me, it is musically interesting that paintings exist on

a canvas with borders. A piece of music unfolds in time and ends in silence. A painting is continually in the present, unaffected by time, yet it is always in the process of ending at each edge of the canvas. A painting, if rectangular, has four endings. It may have a frame around it, which further complicates the concept of endings. Certainly the wall around the frame is an overwhelming irrelevance that must be blocked out by the viewer, like extraneous sounds during a concert. Endings in the visual arts and music can suggest varying degrees of completeness: a smooth sculpture that leaves some part of stone in its natural confusion; a painting that allows drips and patches of naked canvas; or a piece of music that vanishes without a conclusive cadence, fades out while repeating or slides into silence. I have tried, in some of my pieces, to let the music drip toward the edge of the temporal canvas and meet the unconcerned white wall of silence.

What about the visual aspects of the endings of book chapters? Is it more satisfying to read one that concludes at the very bottom of a page, or one that makes you turn once more and then ends rudely near the very top of the next page?

# LEVELS OF DISSONANCE

To MANY LISTENERS, the word *dissonance* suggests an unpleasant arrangement of notes: acerbic, stinging, bitter. In truth, the emotional range of dissonance is infinite. Without dissonance, music—virtually all music in every style —is like language without verbs or adjectives. (Try writing that way.)

Dissonance exists on many musical levels, not only the note-against-note variety. The most common (or "common practice") note-against-note dissonances are so well-known to musicians that they have names. All of these simple dissonances are non-harmonic (or "non-chord") tones—pitches that are foreign to the harmony of the moment. There are non-harmonic tones that pass by in scale formation; these are known as "passing tones". Passing tones are like people who briefly obstruct your view in the theater by moving to one side or the other; or like an advertisement that comes in the mail and is slipped into the trash unopened. Another common note-against-note dissonance is called the "neighboring tone"—which may be an upper or lower neighbor. As the name suggests, a chord-tone may briefly go up or down to visit a dissonant neighboring non-chord tone. This is very much like borrowing the sugar from your upstairs neighbor in an apartment building or, in a slightly more dissonant example, your downstairs neighbor banging on your floor with a broom to get you to turn down the stereo. The suspension is a more important and expressive non-harmonic tone. Suspensions are tones that are held while the rest of the harmony moves on; at the moment of suspension, these tones are non-harmonic. Then they move on to join the other notes in the new harmony, which is called the moment of resolution. When you get your coat caught in the front door as you are leaving the house, your coat is like a suspension. When you pull it out and continue on your way, the suspension has been resolved. The opposite of a suspension is a dissonance called an anticipation. This is a note that moves on to the next harmony before the others, like your peeking your head into a room before you enter.

Beyond the level of note-against-note dissonance, we have harmonic dissonance. This refers to an entire chord that, on its own, may seem consonant, but in context is dissonant. You only need two chords to establish such a relationship, just as you need two people to establish any hierarchy, such as taller, prettier, smarter, older or meaner. Such dissonance is common in real life: a violinist puts on a red dress and shows up at the concert to discover her pianist in an orange dress. Both dresses were consonant at home; together on stage they are dissonant.

Another level of harmonic dissonance is *functional* dissonance. This refers to a harmony which, even when sounded alone, is dissonant because it requires resolution to another, more stable sounding, harmony. It is the chord's function in music to create tension and then to resolve, just as it is a therapist's function to bring out troubles and then aid in their resolution. The most dissonant conventional (common practice) harmony is known as the diminished seventh chord. Because it consists of three equally spaced intervals (minor thirds), it has no top, middle or bottom when played out of context. This symmetry creates tension and suspense. The diminished seventh chord is ready to spring into action and may resolve naturally into eight different keys. A good tennis player is like a diminished seventh chord: the body symmetrically poised, not leaning one way or the other, standing balanced, ready to move to the right or left, forward or back.

Structural dissonance is the next level. It is a dissonance of musical sections within a larger framework. A modulation to a new key within a movement is a simple example of structural dissonance. If a piece is in the key of F Major, we call that key the tonic — it is the home key, where we begin and expect to return. When the music modulates into another key, such as C Major or D Minor, that is a structural dissonance which needs to be resolved by a return to the tonic. If the new key is further away from the F Major tonic harmonically, such as A-flat Major or D-flat Major, then the dissonance is more pronounced. The length of time spent in the non-tonic key also adds to the level of dissonance. This is very much like taking a trip away from home. When you leave Manhattan to visit your grandmother in the Bronx, that is a mild structural dissonance. The dissonance increases if you stay overnight and becomes quite intense if you move in. If you travel to Tokyo, the structural dissonance is greater, and you would need to stay longer than overnight to make the trip worthwhile, just as a visit to a distant key requires time to establish itself. The beep of the alarm clock that startles you awake is itself only a non-harmonic dissonance, but the change from dreaming to making coffee in the kitchen is a major structural dissonance, to be resolved that night after the late show. In non-tonal music (music that is not in a key and has no pitch center), structural dissonance may be a matter of register, timbre, density or level of sustained harmonic dissonance. This would be akin to your walking around your house on tiptoes for six hours rather than taking a trip, or perhaps speaking in a high voice during the afternoon and using your normal voice again starting at sunset.

The concept of structural dissonance may be intensified, bringing us to a new level: contextual dissonance. At this level, sections of music may seem dissonant merely because they are in some way out of place. This is a particularly modern idea that may involve radical changes of tempo, mood or even compositional style. Musical quotes or paraphrases from other works of another era, either in discreet sections or in collage, may provide startling contextual dissonances. Composers who have pioneered the use of this kind of dissonance include George Rochberg, Luciano Berio, George Crumb and Peter Maxwell Davies. In Rochberg's *Eden: Out of Time, Out of Space*, we suddenly find a fleeting ragtime quote in the midst of an atonal environment. Ironically, since the conventionally "dissonant" harmonies have been established as the norm, the simple ragtime quote is emotionally, psychologically dissonant.

The psychological dissonance achieved by Rochberg is commonly experienced in real life. I have felt it when trying to compose music in my ninth floor apartment, when suddenly I am aware of a car stopped at the corner outside my building, blaring music from its radio. This unexpected music intrudes violently on my thought process before the light changes and the car drives away, its music trailing into the distance.

Think of the dissonances in our daily thoughts, and the levels become clear, immediate: the sudden thought that wakes you in the middle of the night; the silly annoyance that you can't get out of your mind; the painful memory that lingers; the lover whose image keeps you from concentrating on your work; the plans and ambitions that may go unrealized.

All of it is dissonance.

# Discovering Simplicity

Typical audience members in America — and many arts presenters, as well — are still afraid of twentieth-century music, although the twenty-first century is upon us. The legacy of the century's early modernism — such as Schoenberg's expressionistic, nightmarish music — lingers vaguely in the minds of many, who dread any "contemporary" music the way I dread the ever popular violent-hero-gets-revenge movies. My intention in this essay is not to defend the early music of this century, as much as I love and admire it, but simply to make a few comments about new music now, and to convey my own thoughts as a composer at the turn of a century.

Those who venture to the concert hall to hear new works in our time will discover that there is little to fear and much to look forward to. Many composers at the turn of the twentieth century are reclaiming their rights to clarity and beauty. Composers have turned away, generally, from complication and pervasive dissonance. The desire to shock is itself considered old-fashioned by many.

But dangers for composers lurk everywhere in this new simplicity: we must be careful to be simple rather than simplistic, pure rather than vapid, innocent rather than immature, clear rather than obvious. We mustn't shy away from richness, which may be complex in nature, but rather from the needlessly complicated.

In a time when challenging ideas may be decried as elitist (as though thinking were somehow reserved for the privileged), and the bottom line is mistaken for a measurement of artistic worth, those of us who wish to search our souls for a living have our work cut out for us. In a world defined by success and failure, poetic ideas are marginalized, ignored. When advertising has become an accepted art form (regardless of its obviously prostitutional nature), when slogans are the poetry of the people, and when our omnipresent pop culture has become an industry based on adolescent voyeurism, we need pure music more than ever.

I believe that people need and want more than fashion and titillation. We will always have the need to recognize mystery, to take time to experience and express it, to discover ideas of beauty. Mystery involves an element of "not knowing", and may be frightening, but not only in the old expressionist way. Beauty, in art and life, is not necessarily pretty.

Composers have always had to discover the techniques of music that can serve their imaginations, and to avoid allowing technique to dictate ideas. (We all know how this can happen with technology that provides such ease of communication that we mistake quick and constant chatter for the thoughtful exchange of ideas.)

Like many of my colleagues, I compose with a less dissonant musical vocabulary than did the early modernists, and I have turned to an even more pure harmonic idiom in my recent music. But this purity embodies, I hope, a kind of "radical innocence"—to borrow a phrase of Yeats. For me, beauty in music—at least in my own, now—has something to do with the sadness implicit in all joy. This has to do with longing, belonging and loneliness. It has to do with the knowledge of the inevitable passing of all that we love, a concept well-suited to musical expression, which necessarily moves in time, blooming and disappearing.

When a piece of music triggers the loops of memory, we simultaneously recognize our commonality and that we are ultimately alone. Our awareness of loneliness and our desire to deny it through love is a great inspiration to create things of beauty. As Yeats put it: "...the soul, remembering its loneliness, shudders in many cradles." The universal shuddering is the music I am trying to find. The closer composers get to that music, the more likely we will not be alone when we listen.

# Serenades, Talk Shows and the Lost Art of Conversation

MUCH OF THE GREAT MUSIC OF THE PAST ENDURES because it gives form and voice to human dramas — dramas that are played out again and again in every generation. The dramatic principal of the sonata provides a set of boundaries within which an infinity of stories may unfold. The stories may have little in common, and yet the sonata principal will provide structure, much as the way rules of order in a courtroom can accommodate — and at best help illuminate — an endless parade of human conflicts from traffic arguments to murder. Not every musical form is quite so flexible as the sonata, however. Those forms that are not dramatic in nature, but rather reflective of a particular lifestyle, may seem like museum pieces. The *serenade* is such a form.

The very thought of serenades brings us back to a time when music fit into society quite differently than it does now. There were, of course, serenades written to entertain the nobility as they dined, much as we now listen to the radio, or to greet a person of stature upon arrival in an outdoor setting. But serenades began as a way for a suitor to gain the attention of his beloved.

Our popular image of serenades comes in great part from operas like *The Marriage of Figaro, Don Giovanni* and *The*

*Barber of Seville.* In the opening of Rossini's *The Barber of Seville,* we get a comic picture of a serenade in action. Fiorello, Count Almaviva's servant, has gathered together a band of musicians to serenade Rosina by accompanying the Count in his profession of love. Rossini manages to give a sense of reality to the scene: Fiorello has to remind the over-sized band of musicians to be very quiet, not to talk — not to disturb the setup and ruin his chances.

But what of the serenade today, in our culture? Is it a serenade when a young man drives up to an apartment building, flips open the trunk of his car to reveal two huge stereo speakers and blasts the neighborhood with a carefully selected love song, awakening not only his girlfriend but several hundred strangers, deafening unsuspecting passersby, setting off car alarms for two blocks, and causing epileptic seizures in small rodents? The word "serenade" comes from *serenus* ...from "serene". According to a music dictionary of 1732, serenades were "evening music usually performed on quiet, pleasant nights." They were deliberately "serene" pieces. However, it is possible that, like the present-day car-stereo blasting episodes, the large wind ensembles commonly used for outdoor serenades disturbed some people who were just trying to sleep on those quiet, pleasant nights.

For those who cannot play an instrument, hi-fi equipment has become the obvious choice for serenading. In Woody Allen's early film *Play it Again, Sam,* Allen's character is expecting his date to come to his apartment, and he wants to create the proper mood with music, to serenade her in order to seduce her, even if subliminally. He struggles with a musical decision: what from his record collection will do the job? Should he impress her with his musical intellect or just set up the background music for a romantic evening? In other words, will it be Bartok quartets or jazz? Finally, he decides to *display* the Bartok, leaving the LP covers conspicuously lying about with carefully arranged nonchalance, and to play the jazz on his turntable. This, he hopes, will strike the perfect balance. His serenade was, to put it mildly, in vain.

Carl Nielsen's *Serenata in vano*, or "Serenade in Vain", is a depiction of a failed musical seduction. Nielsen wrote about this odd serenade: "The work is a humorous trifle. First the gentlemen play in a somewhat chivalrous and showy manner to lure the fair one out onto the balcony, but she does not appear. Then they play a slightly languorous strain (the *poco adagio*), but that doesn't have any effect either. Since they have played in vain, they don't care a straw, and shuffle off home to the strains of the little final march, which they play for their own amusement."

Nielsen based this whole concept on Mozartian models —complete with a march movement, played while marching to the appointed serenade location. We know that Leopold, Mozart's father, complained later in life of being unable to participate in the marches because his memory was failing, for at that time the musicians played marches from memory, not reading from little wire music stands attached to their instruments as is common in bands today. Even cellists could march in bands of serenading players, because cellos could be fitted with rings to support a neck strap, like a guitar or bassoon. A neck strap would have solved the problem in another famous Woody Allen scene, where a marching cellist plays two notes sitting in a chair on the street, then picks up his cello and chair and runs after the band, only to sit down again and play another two notes while the band marches on.

In Mozart's day, serenades were performed at about 9 P.M. *Notturnos* were performed at around 11 P.M. Wind ensembles were excellent for outdoor performances, since they were louder than strings and could be heard throughout the Town Square. In our day, a serenade can be heard throughout the country if it is broadcast on the radio. You can phone certain pop radio stations and dedicate a song to whomever you like and hope that your beloved is listening, or you can call and ask him or her to tune in. The radio stations also allow you to deliver a brief verbal message by phone, which is broadcast along with the hit tune you have chosen to dedicate. The serenadee was sure to hear the wind ensemble in eighteenth-century Vienna, along with everyone in the neighborhood. The radio serenade is heard by millions of people, but, unlike the outdoor performance, the listeners have chosen to tune in. Yet it is hardly an improvement in the art of serenading from the point of view of imagination and personal effort.

The tradition of wind ensembles playing for serenades flourished in Mozart's lifetime. Before 1782, music for wind ensembles was not very significant in Vienna. Wind ensembles were played in taverns and at military events, but the only member of the court who seemed interested in wind music was a fellow named Prince Schwarzenberg. Mozart, who had composed wind divertimentos for the Archbishop in

Salzburg, hoped to influence the Viennese court—to convince them of the beauty of wind music, or *Harmoniemusik*, as it was called. He composed a wind sextet, the typical size of a wind piece, but only a year later, the Emperor decided that *Harmonie* pieces should be octets only. Mozart quickly responded by composing a new octet for winds in C Minor (K.388) and by adding two oboes to the sextet. Meanwhile, the Emperor had decided that original compositions for winds were not as interesting as opera transcriptions for winds. In response, Mozart whipped up a transcription of his *Abduction from the Seraglio*—but to Mozart's great shock and dismay, the court oboist had already written a transcription of that opera, and so Mozart's was redundant. As far as we know, Mozart never got a wind ensemble piece into the imperial library.

Mozart composed the remarkable *Gran Partita*—the Serenade in B-flat for 12 winds and contrabass—before the serenades mentioned above, when he had just moved from Salzburg to Munich, and would soon be on his way to Vienna. In Munich, he worked on the opera *Idomeneo* for the Bavarian Court Theater that employed the very finest wind players of the time—some of whom Mozart had met earlier in Mannheim. He seems to have had these remarkable players in mind as inspiration when composing the B-flat Serenade, even though he completed the work in Vienna. The first performance may actually have been at Mozart's own wedding: and it would have proved a great choice, indeed, for the occasion. The first known performance of at least some of the piece was at the 1784 benefit concert for Anton Stadler, the brilliant clarinetist for whom Mozart composed both the clarinet quintet and the concerto. Mozart wrote the serenade for an unprecedented group of thirteen instrumentalists, including two oboes, two clarinets and two basset horns as the treble instruments, two pairs of horns in different keys—which permitted a greater range of harmonic possibilities—and two bassoons and a double bass for the foundation. If he had waited one more year to compose the serenade, Mozart would have had the option of using a rudimentary version of the newly devised contrabassoon, which had been recently brought into Vienna by Theodor Lotz. But having no such creature, Mozart had to use a string instrument—the double bass—to provide the sixteen-foot pitch, an octave below the bassoons.

The slow movement of the B-flat Serenade is one of the most famous adagios in instrumental music. In the play *Amadeus* by Peter Shaffer, Salieri, court composer to Emperor Joseph II, describes the painful beauty of the opening of the *Adagio*. It is such exquisite music, the Salieri of the play believes, that he could never hope to write something that approaches it. Shaffer's Salieri declares that in this music he had heard "a voice of God."

Considered by many musicians to be the most beautiful movement of any serenade, the *Adagio* is composed like a scene from an opera. It is not a solo aria, but an operatic trio, suggesting a conversation among three eloquent poets, played by the first oboe, the first clarinet and the first basset horn. The three voices connect, intertwining to form one long melody, which sometimes splits into three aspects of a single melodic thought. The overlapping is carefully controlled. Each instrument contributes a specific aspect to the design, so that form and content are one, and so that melodic function and instrumental color are at all times unified, inseparable.

The elegance of this adagio, and of Mozart's music generally, reminds us that it comes from an age of manners. It further reminds us that ours is *not* an age of manners. This music was born in a society that held conversation to be an art. It was an art that was practiced, like the piano. Conversation for pleasure and edification, imagine that! It involved the careful balancing of viewpoints, the sifting of ideas and opinions just for the sheer joy of it, for the delight of the interchange and in the pursuit of mutual enlightenment. In Mozart's music, we can experience that rarified atmosphere of manners that allowed for courteous and cordial conversation.

In America today, especially in politics and on television, what passes for conversation is merely the exchange of set, immovable opinions. Verbal jousting and sound bites prevail. Interviews are far more common than conversations. Artful conversation, especially for the sheer pleasure of speaking the language well, is dead, even though so-called "talk shows" are the rage. Millions of Americans tune in to latenight television to hear rude and senseless chatter, endless self-promotion, juvenile innuendo and simplistic political satire. The latest craze in American daytime television is the confrontation and confession type of program, in which people scream at each other, argue thoughtlessly and savagely about their private lives, and physically accost each other when words fail, which they inevitably do.

What would Haydn, Mozart, Descartes or Benjamin Franklin think of the screaming and yelling that permeates the entertainment industry today on commercial television and radio? How would they react to the promotional propaganda that is passed off as "talk", or the lopsided interviews (where the interviewer is obviously uninformed about the guest) that we have begrudgingly come to accept as sophisticated conversation on public television? What kind of music would reflect all this yelling, bullying, whining and endless plugging?

Is it any wonder that so many young people who grow up in this atmosphere do not readily relate to Mozart's music? The child who sees society's official role models on television engaged in empty, self-important howling, who hears only righteous opinions and thinly disguised marketing at every turn, may have trouble relating to elegance and poetic expression.

We need Mozart and his eloquent serenades to bring a nearly forgotten kind of beauty into our lives, to remind us of the meaning of *delight*, to lead us back to an idea of elegance and grace—and to instruct us in the important art of conversation. We are in desperate need of conversation; we have enough posturing and propaganda. Let Mozart serenade and seduce us, his willing listeners, with grace, dignity, humanity and—hardest to come by—serenity of mind.

# COMPOSING FOR CHILDREN

WHEN I WAS 10 YEARS OLD, I did my first concert tour. I played the piano and narrated Prokofiev's *Peter and the Wolf* for every class in my elementary school. It was such a hit that my school (Cornwell Avenue School in West Hempstead, Long Island) sent me to a few other local elementary schools to do my one-boy version of *Peter and the Wolf.*

While I enjoyed performing for other kids, the reason for the tour was that I was obsessed with Prokofiev's piece. I played it over and over at home, and I would give unsolicited impromptu performances of it wherever a piano might be found. In those better days of public school education, there was a piano in every room of the school, except, of course, the bathrooms. Each classroom sported an identical upright with a light tan stain on the wood. They were kept reasonably in tune and, except for cigarette holes burned into some of the keys, were in decent condition. So a tour to every class was easy to accomplish, easier than touring to many professional concert venues around the country where it is impossible to predict what condition the piano will be in. (Although a tan upright with cigarette holes would be considered unusable by any self-respecting pianist over ten years old.)

After the *Peter and the Wolf* tour, I composed my own stories with music and played them for my classmates. One major project, which I could not complete, was an opera about being unjustly imprisoned ("*The Prison Opera*", I called it). It was inspired by a 60's protest song that I can no longer remember. Deep down, I wanted to compose my own Peter and the Wolf, or perhaps it would be more accurate to say that I wished I had written it. Other storytelling pieces made their way into my heart during my childhood. Stravinsky's *Story of a Soldier* left me reeling with excitement, and it eventually replaced the Prokofiev work as my favorite story piece.

The joy of telling stories with music has remained very important to me as a grown-up composer, and I have written quite a few such works, prolonging, in a sense, my first tour indefinitely. My pieces *Marita and Her Heart's Desire*, *Sharehi* (*Dancing Stories*), *Little Red Riding Hood*, *Goldilocks and the Three Bears*, and *The Purple Palace* all tell stories, some brand new, some very familiar.

The integration of story and music is an important part of a healthy childhood. It is obvious that we learn and grow by hearing stories in which characters learn and grow. Music, when it is composed with care and skill, adds emotional layers that take the listener beyond the somewhat circumscribed vocabulary of childhood tales. The warmth and innocence of Peter's theme in *Peter and the Wolf* is combined with a clever modulation of keys, suggesting a restlessness that perfectly matches his character and behavior. When Peter "opens the gate and goes out into the bright green meadow", we can sense in the slippery change of keys that he is not where he should be, even if we have no musical training at all. (I did not understand that consciously when I performed the work in my elementary school.) The listener knows a lot about Peter before the story unfolds. In Stravinsky's *Story of a Soldier*, the music is a dazzling cut-and-paste pastiche presented in brief vivid episodes, the whole suggesting a story depicted in a stained glass window. This intensifies the story's spirituality, while giving it some distance and objectifying it. While Stravinsky's piece is not specifically "targeted" (as we now unfortunately say) for children, it appeals to them as much as to adults. One of the most discouraging developments of our marketing-driven world is the obsession with identifying the "target" audience. While there are musical stories obviously better suited to children or adults, the best pieces work on several levels, and may be thoroughly enjoyed by everyone. When a composer or author is too focused on a specific age group, the result is usually a loss of dimension, of layering. Even when a story is very simple and simply told, it is possible and desirable for the musical aspects of the work to be sophisticated emotionally and technically. In many commercial musical works for children, the music is "dumbed-down" and is quite condescending. This kind of "product" is a far cry from art. It does not edify or inspire, but merely entertains and keeps kids busy (usually with videos), and it is part of an industry geared toward giving parents a break. Usually, the "visuals" that accompany such entertainment are, likewise, unimaginative and play into cheap stereotypes that send unfortunate subversive messages, such as the Victoria's Secret-style Indian maiden of Disney's *Pocahontas*.

No cartoon of *Peter and the Wolf* (and there have been many) will ever be the image for the work. In its pure musical form, it allows boys to picture themselves as Peter. When Louise Gikow wrote the story for *Marita and Her Heart's Desire*, she wanted to give little girls such a character with whom to identify. When I conceived the piece, I wanted to accomplish something in musical storytelling that was missing in *Peter and the Wolf*, although I had not, at first, figured out what that would be. I soon realized that Prokofiev's wonderful themes are presented in a variety of actions, but the work is not particularly contrapuntal. This gave me a cause: to create a storytelling piece in which the systematic building up of contrapuntal textures would be the point, the game, the fun of the piece. To this end, Louise created a story around my contrapuntally-designed musical structure. Each character and theme would be introduced separately, yet each would be combined with every other in a variety of musical textures that further the plot. My compositional task became an elaborate game of creating themes (for Marita, the cat, the rat, the dog and the mouse) that did not suggest counterpoint, so that when the themes were later combined, there would be a sense of surprise. As the tale unfolds, the listener begins to suspect that each new theme will fit into the puzzle, and this creates a kind comic musical suspense.

For a musical story piece to be artistically satisfying, it must be conceived musically first. It should not be a story with music merely tacked on here and there. This is why in my musical settings of *Goldilocks and the Three Bears*, I have restructured the story. First, it was necessary to introduce the bears one at a time, so that each could have an identifying theme, like a *leitmotif* in opera. The bears' themes could then be used to build an entertaining and intriguing musical form that is suggested by the original tale, but missing in the story's structure. This is why I have Goldilocks spotting each bear in the woods *before* she gets to their house. Their themes and their contrapuntal nature, which includes Goldilocks's own tune in the mix, become the whole musical point of the piece. (I have also updated the scene just a bit, for I believe that the more immediate a story is, the more real it seems, and the more real it seems, the funnier are its impossibilities.) The idea of counterpoint for kids has been a significant goal in all my recent story pieces. Listening to counterpoint within a story context, children are naturally and easily engaged in a musical learning process that opens their minds to rich artistic experiences. Without any extra effort, they find themselves able to identify multiple simultaneous independent parts. In the contrapuntal climax of *Marita and Her Heart's Desire*, five themes are presented simultaneously, as Marita, the cat, the rat, the dog and the mouse enter Harper's Department Store together.

Composing for children (and their parents) has led me to explore the fundamental issues of musical structure and syntax in a new light. Far from leading to musical simplification, it has led me to a refinement of language and technique, which has taught me more than any other musical endeavor. I have opened the gate and gone out into the bright green meadow.

# TEACHING COMPOSITION NOW

THE STORY GOES that a young, aspiring composer cornered Mozart and demanded to know, "How should I learn the art of composition?"

Mozart answered, "Don't compose a thing until you have studied the great works carefully, until you have understood the methods of the masters. Wait until you are ready, and then, and only then, you may try your hand at composing." The student, shocked and disappointed, said, "But Maestro, certainly you did not proceed in that way." Mozart answered, "I never asked such a question either."

Those who want to compose usually shoot first and ask questions later.

If you want to write words, first you have to talk. If you want to compose, first you must play an instrument. There is no right moment after that to begin. Composing must start before the composition studies can begin. If not, the first assignment from a teacher will fix that: "Compose something and call me when you like what you've done."

Composing is like writing prose or poetry, except that we are not all immersed in music as a way of thinking early enough for it to seem natural. Mozart's father, Leopold, wanted his children to be virtuosi and, as early as possible, began their musical instruction. Even as a small child, Mozart would forget his meals when absorbed in music. He would only be interested in playing games if there were a musical accompaniment provided. Certainly Suzuki would support that idea. When music is a natural part of family life from early on, it is far more likely that talent will out.

Just as with writing in English, composing can be honed, refined and developed with guidance and nurturing. A good teacher can be very helpful, but what does a composition teacher do in this age of cultural hyper-eclecticism when an aspiring composer is most likely overwhelmed by an infinity of musical styles and influences?

A good teacher deals differently with each student. The course of study should depend, to a great extent, on what the student needs. Some composition teachers insist on a rigorous study of past techniques. They might teach "species counterpoint", an approach to counterpoint based on a theoretical understanding of Renaissance polyphony (which is an analytical rather than a compositional way of thinking), in order to instill a sense of order and discipline. Many teachers today put their students through this exercise, which I feel to be a delay in the study of composition. Even Bach considered that kind of teaching, and species counterpoint in particular, to be old-fashioned.

How did Bach teach? Bach taught his students the contemporary grammar of music: how to compose a good bass line; how to build harmonies and progressions above it, using consistent voice-leading in the individual parts; how to further liberate the individual lines from the harmonies to create graceful melodic contours; how to intensify the independence of the lines in order to construct counterpoint. For Bach, counterpoint was an organic process. It was built up from the harmonic foundation. Harmony was the tree trunk, contrapuntal lines were the individual branches, and fugue, the highest level of contrapuntal development, was the fruit.

That was a time when musicians in a given country shared an aesthetic, a common language, which composers grew up hearing and intended to employ. Bach could teach *proper* voice-leading. The word "proper" has virtually no meaning in the art any more, and understandably so.

In Mozart's day, too, a composer who taught could rightly assume that the student wished to learn a particular method or set of techniques. There were rules of harmony just as there are rules of grammar. Rules were not a question of style, for style was not a question. Rules were helpful; they explained how the game was played. As a child, Mozart wrote minuets and marches modeled on those that he played on the piano and heard performed. As he matured, there was no question of his individual voice, but rather the opposite was valued: the ability to do things properly. An individual voice would naturally arise, of course, but it would be the inevitable result of talent, and was not considered an end in itself.

If we consider even one facet of composition from earlier times, the *cadence*, for example, it is clear how far we have come from the concept of shared aesthetics. Until the early twentieth century, cadences did not have to be unique to a given composition. Quite the contrary is true now. While endings of works in the eighteenth century may be *emotion-*

*ally* satisfying or not, the actual harmonies of a cadence were a matter of grammar, of what is called "common practice." The types of cadences used for phrase endings, movement endings, and for the endings of whole pieces, were so commonly employed that they were more like punctuation marks than part of the "text" of the music. These formula cadences have names: semi-cadence, full cadence, deceptive cadence, Phrygian cadence, plagal cadence, and so forth. Furthermore, the dissonances that may be used to intensify the penultimate harmonies also were codified: suspension, anticipation, cambiata, pedal point, to name a few.

Today, composers cannot employ any of these cadences, with or without their attendant permutations, without the result sounding like an historical reference, a kind of Neoclassicism, or just an anachronism. The mere rhythmic resonance and contour of traditional cadences, even in the complete absence of the expected tonal harmony, may be understood as "derivative" (a naughty word) and anachronistic. This is partly the result of the dissolution of common practice tonality generally, of course, but it is also because of a change of psychology, of the *purpose* of *art music.* "Art music", as opposed to music in the popular culture, has become far more personal than communal, confessional rather than congregational, private (in nature) rather than public. The absence of such a simple concept as a common practice cadence speaks volumes about the state of contemporary composition.

Today, most music schools and departments teach harmony itself as if it were only an historical concept. It is as though there *were at one time* principals and procedures, but *now* there are none. Harmony — a fundamental pillar of musical architecture — is, for many composition students, a theoretical subject more relevant to musicology than to contemporary thought. Many graduating composers are led to believe that every good composer must have a unique, personal harmonic language, or they are merely imitators. To complicate matters, listeners — including professional musicians and critics — might think less of a work by a composer if the music seems in any way "too" familiar, or if the harmonic language reminds them too easily of another composer's. This leads composition students to conclude that there is no way to judge the quality of one's work with regard to harmony (and by extension, anything) other than how *unlike* other music it is. This attitude makes a student feel righteous and protective about any divergence from a norm or standard. Righteousness usually leads to closed-mindedness. It is all based on insecurity. And who would not be insecure faced with the task of creating art in a professional artistic environment that seems to favor the *unfamiliar* in the midst of a society that craves the *familiar*. No wonder composers are often defensive and, quite frequently, prone to spouting complicated explanations and justifications of the techniques and language of their music.

A good composition teacher must break through this defensive wall, which often exists even in students, or try to prevent its development. Yet, many composition teachers give the impression that it is all just a matter of personal taste. One merely has to decide what one likes (or the student could speed things up by liking the teacher's music and becoming a disciple). Ironically, this is the same stance as the average philistine who declares: "I may not know what's good, but I know what I like." What is missing from this picture is fundamental: musical structures and techniques have meaning, and so the techniques used to create music must serve a point of view. In fact, they will support a point of view, even if the composer is not consciously aware of it, or even if he or she denies it or proclaims the opposite to be true. It is not merely a matter of "I know what I like."

If a student wears a Nazi swastika because he thinks it looks "cool", someone should explain to him what it means, and they should discuss how people will react to it. While this example might seem extreme, it is a useful way to illustrate the issue of "taste" (or "fashion") without *meaning*. A good composition teacher must help the student become aware of the implications, content and context of compositional techniques. Debussy's famous proclamation that there is no theory, only pleasure, and that pleasure is the law, was fine and true for a rebel composing in the restrictive atmosphere of the Paris Conservatoire—especially a rebel who was already educated, an advanced composer and a genius. But we cannot approach every student as if he or she were a genius. If we do, we can expect a world full of arrogant but incompetent composers, insisting on their personal vision over all objections, serving not the art of music nor the community, but only their own image of themselves marching in a procession of geniuses. All this, while Rome burns. The study of composition should be the unification of technique and meaning in the service of the art. The art must loom larger than its practitioners — especially in the minds of its practitioners.

Benjamin Britten loved to recount the story of a lesson he had taken with the composer Frank Bridge. The older composer found the young man's sketches to be awkwardly composed and told him so. Young Ben Britten protested, "But I meant for it to sound that way." "Well you *oughtn't* to have meant that!" Bridge retorted.

Today, a student might compose any combination of tones followed by any other combination. We live in a brave new world of anything goes. Unlike previous times, we now have the entire world of music, past and present, at our fingertips through recordings and printed scores. We live in a global museum. Browsing through one of the compact disc superstores, or on the internet, one can find music from many centuries and countries — all of it, except the current popular styles, crammed into the Classical Section, of course. A young student is quite likely to write in a pastiche of styles, perhaps innocently and accidentally combining sounds from different centuries and countries. It is just as likely, however, that the young student will compose something after the manner of Mozart, Chopin or Scriabin as well as Bartok, Steve Reich, or John Williams. There is no predicting what an aspiring composer's frame of reference might be. A teacher must guide a student emotionally as well as technically. A young composer needs to discover not an individual voice — that can only come with experience — but a point of view, at least for the moment. Even if a student accidentally stumbles upon an interesting mix of diverse musical styles, the teacher must help the student identify the influences and techniques. A young composer needs to know how to distinguish and select ideas from the dizzying swirl of possibilities, and what techniques might possibly suit those ideas that have been chosen.

During the many years of my teaching composition at the Juilliard School's Pre-College Division, and in my teaching for the Composers Apprentice Program that I created for the Chamber Music Society of Lincoln Center in 1990, I have developed and adapted exercises that stimulate focused musical thinking, encourage creativity and foster discipline through serious playfulness. These exercises unite technique with meaning without forcing the issue. I believe there is more to be gained from the kinds of exercises described below than from the two typical extremes of teaching, the overly controlled species counterpoint approach and the hands-off, anything goes approach.

One very productive exercise (or game) is the spontaneous keyboard conversation. The teacher improvises a brief phrase of music on the piano; the student must answer the phrase, beginning with the exact note or notes that ended the teacher's phrase. The teacher then picks up on the final notes played by the student and continues. They improvise together in this manner, building a piece together, each trying to make sense of what the other has played. Soon, it becomes clear that a responding phrase might be a *continuation* or a *contrast*; it may *affirm* or *contradict*, *extend* or *divert*. The teacher's improvised phrases will communicate aspects of the art without having to explain or describe them. Any musical techniques or ideas that the teacher wishes the student to confront are simply introduced by the teacher in the improvisation, no comments necessary. The good student will learn a great deal from this in a purely musical way, by ear and by feel: the best way. Afterward, a discussion of what took place, or an attempt to write some of it down, might be enlightening.

Another version of this exercise, which I have used not only to teach composition but music history and theory as well, is to play the same spontaneous conversation, but to begin with a phrase from a famous piece of music. This is one way to learn from master composers by "collaborating" with them. The teacher might start with the opening of a prelude by Bach, the first bars of Beethoven's *Waldstein Sonata*, a madrigal by Gesualdo or the opening bassoon solo of Stravinsky's *Rite of Spring*. The game is the same, except that now we have an existing piece of repertoire with which to compare our improvisations. Responding only to the first phrase in this game is enough to learn a great deal. Writing out the responses, instead of improvising them, is an intensification of this game.

One of my favorite ways to help students discover their own musical personalities is to give the following assignment: *compose your own leitmotif.* A *leitmotif* is an identifying fragment, a brief musical gesture, phrase or theme that signals (as in a Wagner opera) the presence of a particular character (such as Wotan) or idea (such as love). This causes a composer to think *past* technique, *past* style, and to proceed directly to *essence.* The student wonders, "If this is about me, what will the energy of the music be, the tempo, the mood, what *personality* should be embodied in this brief musical idea?" Since we are real people—not fictional characters who symbolize aspects of humanity—*no leitmotif* can do us justice. The effort to create such a motif, and the composition of different versions, will teach us a great deal about music and ourselves.

Just as painters apprenticed themselves to masters, learned the master's style and even painted with and for him, composers can benefit from models. However, the way this is practiced is of the utmost importance. It can be stifling or liberating, depending upon the approach. My suggestion is *not to imitate* a great composer but to *pretend to be* that composer. This is not mere semantics. If you are asked to imitate someone, you will end up with superficial parody. If you are asked to pretend you are that person, you will identify with them profoundly. Imitation may be the sincerest form of flattery, but it is also demeaning and often feels like academic work, a sensation that a composer should avoid when writing music. To pretend to be someone else turns the whole endeavor into theater, gives the "actor" a feeling of genius, and liberates the student from any hint of academicism. "I am not a student, I'm Shostakovich."

Another way to learn from a model is to combine analysis with composition in a way that I call "transfusion". First, the student examines a piece—let's say it is Beethoven's Opus 95 String Quartet. The student charts a "map" of the piece that includes its general shape and significant details: phrase lengths, melodic contour, texture, dynamics, modulations, and so on. We end up with a kind of drawing of the music without musical notation. Then comes the transfusion: the student composes new music that closely follows the map of Opus 95. The student has borrowed the drama of the piece, its scenario, without its characters or dialogue. It can be a great lesson.

A teacher of composition should also challenge a student to experiment with process. Students who compose at the piano should try composing away from the instrument. Those who compose in their heads might find sitting at the piano and improvising gives them access to another part of their musical imagination. I think it is important to know what it feels like to compose both ways. I often encourage a student to use both techniques within a single composition. For example, try improvising at the keyboard for several hours and select something from the improvisation as the primary idea of a work. Then, leave the keyboard and imagine the piece as if dreaming about it. Write out this unplayed (but clearly heard) music, only returning to the piano after a significant amount of silent composing has been accomplished. The opposite approach involves getting into a trance (as Leonard Bernstein recommended) by lying on the floor or (as I prefer) a couch. Imagine that you are in a concert hall, seated in the audience. Musicians enter and perform a work that you find thrilling or beautiful. Can you remember this music when you go to the piano? Can you play it? By experimenting with sound, as physical reality through improvisation in *alternation* with sound as daydream, we expand our capacity to think in music, to pay attention to our ideas, to imagine new music. When improvisation at the piano and imagining music in silence start to feel the same, the composer has reached a new level of creative ability.

These exercises are paths to a single destination: the understanding that technique serves the imagination. When a composer has managed to fully realize that it is the mind, not devices, that makes music, more meaningful music will be made. A fugue, although potentially a high order of musical thinking, can be dull and meaningless if it is a demonstration of fugal technique. To be meaningful, the fugue must come about because a composer has a message, a purpose, for which fugue is the perfect vehicle. Think of the inventor who spends a year building a grand piano and, when it is done, tries to drive it down Main Street. The great received techniques, structures and devices of music are like equipment for a journey. They are valuable if a composer takes that journey. They are meaningless, or at best nostalgic, if they are merely on display.

Sometimes a musical technique evolves to represent a particular worldview and may completely disappear when that view is no longer important in society. Think of the chorale cantata. This is a concept, evolved and perfected by Johann Sebastian Bach, in which a pre-existing hymn melody, a *cantus firmus*, permeates all aspects, vocal and instrumental, of a cantata. The *cantus firmus* provides the spiritual and technical unity of the work. The chorale cantata, like its sister device, the chorale prelude, may support a variety of textures, but one stands out as a perfect example of form embodying metaphor. That texture, well known to choral singers and organists, presents the *cantus firmus* in slow motion against continuously quick-moving voices. The majestically paced *cantus firmus* may appear in half and whole notes in the soprano voices supported by high trumpets, for example, while the alto, tenor, and bass voices, together with the remaining instruments, rush about in a flurry of sixteenth notes. The *cantus firmus* represents the divine; the other parts represent the human. When sung by sopranos with high trumpets, we picture Baroque paintings with angels crowded in the clouds at the top of the canvas, hovering over the mortals below. The cantus firmus moves slowly, clearly symbolizing eternity, faith, truth. The other parts scurry about, for life on earth is short; it is a busy, bustling world of hardships and temptations. As professional music liberated itself from the church, the chorale cantata and chorale prelude died out. The technique was so successful in conveying its metaphor that it could not survive in a secular compositional environment. The concept was revived suddenly, and singularly, by Ludwig van Beethoven in his String Quartet Opus 132, in the *Heiliger Dankgesang* (Holy Song of Thanksgiving) movement (discussed in the essay *Innovation or Renovation*). Beethoven needed the metaphor to convey his state of mind, and he wanted, as well, the power of its association to Bach. The concept of the chorale cantata/chorale prelude remains associated with Bach to this day and, despite its occasional use in religious oratorios in various styles, has not seen a significant revival.

Not long ago, I found the chorale cantata/chorale prelude concept in a startling new context, given a new lease on life. It was not in a piece of music, but in a dance by Merce

Cunningham. The stage was full of dancers rushing, spinning and leaping about the stage in various patterns while Merce Cunningham himself, at nearly four times the age of some of the dancers, slowly and majestically made his way across the stage on a severe diagonal. As I watched, I was not thinking about chorale cantatas or preludes, or anything Baroque. I found Cunningham's *adagio*, almost weightless walk, so peaceful and purposeful, more gripping, more powerful than all the virtuoso dancing going on around him. He was a master in the midst of disciples, a prophet surrounded by his people; he was divine, they were human. They tried, he just was.

As I left the theater, I overheard a few young dancers in the audience complaining that Merce Cunningham had put himself in the piece because he could not admit that he could no longer dance, that he was old, that he was not the star performer anymore. As I walked home, it became clearer and clearer to me that the Baroque metaphor had been reborn. Merce Cunningham was, in this work, the physical embodiment of a *cantus firmus*, a rock of faith, and his dancers, busy mortals all, were full of ambition — with a world of hardship and temptation ahead of them.

# WARNING:

## THE SIDE EFFECTS OF MUSIC EDUCATION

THROUGHOUT America, public school music programs have been downsized or completely eliminated. Recently, the crisis has finally become so severe that parents, and even politicians, are finally calling for reparations. Psychologists, sociologists, mayors, senators and school chancellors are all declaring that music is an important part of education. Why is it important? Most often, the answer will be that music is important because of its side effects: it promotes spatial awareness, abstract and mathematical thinking, physical coordination and self-esteem. Furthermore, it is a way to learn about diverse cultures and historical periods, and it teaches children to cooperate with each other through group rehearsals and performance. It also keeps children busy after school hours.

It turns out that aspirin, long thought to be good only for temporary relief from headaches and for fever reduction, also thins the blood, thereby helping to prevent heart attacks. Researchers have made many people happy with the news that red wine, in moderate doses, is good for the circulatory system. They have also informed the public that one glass of red wine makes it easier for students to study for exams, while two glasses make it harder. No studies have revealed what three glasses will do. Nicotine, it turns out, can help you lose weight, and it is not — as previously supposed — due to the fact that one's mouth is busy smoking rather than eating. Garlic fights off two out of three diseases, placing it just ahead of broccoli as an alternative prevention food, and it now seems clear that real butter is better than margarine as an impediment to cancer. The best news of all is that laughter is good for longevity, and so researchers are encouraging people to look on the lighter side, if only for health reasons.

America is obsessed with side effects. A side effect of this obsession is that we have improved peripheral vision, but we cannot see what is right in front of us. I am a lover of red wine and garlic, but I confess that it is purely an issue of sensual pleasure. (Some red wines, by the way, taste a lot better than others, though they will have equal medicinal effect.) If it were shown that red wine had no healthful effects, would restaurants close their wine cellars? If music had no effect on children's math scores and the like, would we then argue that it should be dropped from the curriculum?

Music's *direct* effects are far more important than its side effects. Music is as fundamental to thought as is mathematics; it does not merely promote abstract thinking, it is one of the *highest forms* of abstract thought; music is not merely good for self-esteem, it sensually, intellectually and emotionally organizes the mind. This is an ancient concept. Plato wrote in *The Republic*: "...rhythm and harmony find their way into the inward places of the soul, on which they mightily fasten..." Pythagoras and his disciples understood music to be the "harmonization of opposites, the unification of disparate things." These ancient definitions of music, which we should broaden to include the arts generally, find resonance in current neuroscience research that defines creative activity in the brain as the merging of reason and intuition. Neuroscientist Antonio R. Damasio has compared the workings of the mind/brain to a musical score. Beethoven, who knew little or no science, sensed the value of the comparison in 1824. He wrote: "I wish you all success in your efforts on behalf of the arts; it is these, together with science, that give us inclines of a higher existence and the hope of attaining it."

When I complete this paragraph, I will pour myself a glass of wine and listen to a recording of Mahler's *Das Lied von der Erde*. I know, without checking the latest research, that it will do my heart good.

# Postscript

## LISTENING TO MY PARROT SING

THE MUSINGS IN THIS BOOK have been restricted to the musical and artistic activities of humans, with a brief detour to discuss the music of whales in order to illuminate the music of a particular human, George Crumb. I feel that this book would not be complete without a brief consideration of an extraordinarily talented creature who happens not to be human: my parrot.

There have been many arguments about whether animals have feelings, even though it is really quite obvious that they do. Simply because a computer can be programmed to seem to feel (or to seem to think), this does not suggest that living beings are merely "seeming". "I know not 'seems'", as Hamlet says.

My parrot, Polly Rhythm, has been my friend for nearly thirty years. When I was fourteen, my family bought the three-month-old green and fluffy little bird (not the first bird in my family by a long stretch), and he is now a not-so-small, mostly green Yellow Fronted Amazon with beautiful blue and red feathers discreetly kept under his green and yellow wing feathers. The dash of red on the tips of his wings has gotten bolder over the years.

Polly Rhythm is a remarkable singer. He can produce a

fine soprano sound: focused, clear and velvety with that steely "ping" for projection, and he has an expressive vibrato. Polly Rhythm has perfect pitch, always singing his favorite highlights on the same notes, well in tune. In many respects, he seems to be more musical than many people.

Some people, upon first hearing him sing operatic roulades, trills and arpeggios or warble in a funky, jazzy way, ask me, "Why do birds imitate? What would be the use of that in his natural habitat?" The question implies that there must be a purpose connected to survival, that the possibility that the bird sings for enjoyment is either unlikely or absurd. It is possible to come up with a variety of reasonable, pseudoscientific answers: he sings to get food; he imitates singing in order to establish a bond with his owner, a musician, for his own protection and to guarantee food; he imitates singing in the hopes of mating with one of the many humans who sing back to him.

But I hear him sing every day, and I know why he sings. It is for sheer pleasure, and to play. Polly Rhythm sings along with recordings, following as closely as possible the mood, the melody, and even the style of the music. He remembers many fragments of melodies and strings them together spontaneously, creating patterns he has not heard. This is normally called improvising when humans do it. He stands up straight and holds his head high when he sings like a coloratura soprano. He gets down, bobs his head and holds his wings out when he sings in a jazzy style. Polly will use a word, usually "hello", as the text, as he makes up a melodic pattern. I have often heard him singing quietly to himself when I am in another room. On such an occasion, I might sneak up to the door of the room he is in, and listen closely without his knowing. He is either practicing or simply amusing himself, and it is quite beautiful to hear.

Why do humans make music? To meet and mate? To bond with neighbors? To get food? Well, all that and very much more. Music is a way of thinking, of feeling, of communicating. Music provokes, charms, courts, reasons, tickles, arouses, plays, lulls, angers, delights, reminds. As much as I enjoy writing and speaking about music, I know that no words can translate the musical experience. My bird would agree.

# INDEX